Evangelicalism
in America

Evangelicalism in America

by
Bruce L. Shelley

WILLIAM B. EERDMANS PUBLISHING COMPANY
GRAND RAPIDS, MICHIGAN

To

Pastor Albert C. Smith, Chaplain Eugene McGee,
Professor James Hatch, and President Vernon Grounds,

*four men who made me
proud to be an evangelical*

Contents

Preface   7

1: What Is Evangelicalism?   13

2: The Rise of Evangelicalism   25

3: Evangelicalism in America   45

4: The Birth of N A E   69

5: N A E: Ministry and Maturity   85

6: American Evangelicalism Today   111

Notes   133

Preface

Nothing is more difficult than publishing an up-to-date book. Time does not hesitate. In our jet age events pile upon events with such breathtaking speed that a book concerned with contemporary Christianity is somewhat dated before it rolls from the presses.

With this fact in view, I thought it best in this volume marking the twenty-fifth anniversary of the National Association of Evangelicals to cast the event into some sort of perspective. That is why I have devoted so many of these limited lines to "evangelicalism yesterday."

Even beyond the time problem, however, this assignment was not an easy one. Much of my difficulty arose from the nature of the subject.

Evangelical Christianity is not a religious organization. It is not primarily a theological system. It is more of a mood, a perspective, and an experience. And "moods" and "perspectives," even those arising from the Christian gospel, have a way of eluding the historian.

The only way I found to keep some control on this modest introduction to evangelical Christianity was to grasp carefully a few basic terms.

I have used "evangelical," as I try to explain in the first chapter, in a rather inclusive way of all Christians who are concerned with that personal experience of Christ that results from the preaching of the Biblical gospel. Evangelicals are "ortho-

dox" Christians in the sense that they accept the cardinal doctrines of historic Protestantism but they are convinced that the
true doctrine of Christ must be followed by a true decision
for Christ.

Occasionally the reader will find "conservative" as a synonym
for "evangelical." This substitute I have justified for reasons of
style. The constant appearance of "evangelical" in the text
would lead to monotony. I have tried to use "conservative,"
however, in doctrinal contexts, for example, where the "evangelical" is contrasted to the "modernist." This use therefore
will appear more often in the later chapters since "evangelicals"
were not "conservative," at least in their evangelistic methods,
in eighteenth-century England or in nineteenth-century America.

The term "fundamentalist" presents special problems because
of the current controversy surrounding the word. I have tried to
use it to designate that wing of American evangelicalism appearing between the turn of our century and the Second World
War which reacted most vigorously to the introduction of "liberalism" into the denominations. The more fundamentalism
stressed the "defense of the faith" the more it was in danger
of preoccupation with its own purity and of losing the evangelical passion to present the gospel to all men. I have therefore used "fundamentalist" to refer to that stream of evangelical Christianity in the first half of the twentieth century which
was diverted by events in the 1920's to extra-church or independent channels.

This means that I recognize the fact that many evangelicals
remained within those denominations—Methodists, Disciples,
Presbyterians, and Baptists—most affected by the modernist/
fundamentalist controversy and that I realize many others are
to be found in those churches more deeply rooted in the Reformation, especially in Lutheran, Reformed, and Mennonite
groups. In short, I do not equate "fundamentalist" with "evangelical."

Perhaps the reader will feel that I have given undue space to interdenominational evangelicalism. This is understandable. The arrangement, however, was dictated by choice and necessity. I did not think it wise to survey the denominations in order because the difficulties in determining the evangelical strength within each of the churches were staggering.

The renewal within American evangelicalism, especially in interdenominational circles, after World War II has received various labels including "neofundamentalism," "the new conservatism" and "neo-evangelicalism." I have settled on "new evangelicalism" not because it is without problems but because the alternatives have more.

One weakness of "new evangelical" is that it is no longer "new." The movement is at least twenty years old. The other difficulty with the term is its connotation. It suggests that the movement embraces all evangelicals except the "old" evangelicals, whoever they may be. The truth is that the so-called "new evangelicalism" is a fresh current within old fundamentalist (and thus interdenominational) channels which seeks to correct certain excesses of fundamentalism and to recover an earlier evangelical witness to society.

With all of its shortcomings, however, the term does point to something real, a revitalized interdenominational evangelicalism in the United States.

One other expression may be added here because it is gaining wider and wider acceptance. In discussions related to the quest of Christian unity the combination "conservative evangelical" often designates all those "evangelical" Christians who refrain from membership in the National Council of Churches, the World Council of Churches and their regional and local bodies. The phrase has the advantage, on the one hand, of recognizing the fact that numbers of "evangelicals" are active in "conciliar ecumenism" and, on the other hand, of avoiding the identification of all "evangelicals" outside the councils with "fundamentalists."

Some explanation is due the reader for the prominent place

given to the National Association of Evangelicals. This volume was undertaken at the request of Mr. Harvey C. Warner, Director of Information for the NAE, and with the approval of the Association's Board of Administration. The Board felt that a work devoted to the evangelical witness in America could help mark the twenty-fifth anniversary of NAE, which fell on April 7, 1967.

The book is in no sense, however, an "authorized" history. The only request made of me was that I submit the manuscript to three readers from NAE ranks for purposes of checking the historical accuracy of material touching the Association. This request I gladly granted. The selection of subject, the organization of material, and the interpretation of events are all my own. Whatever weaknesses and errors one finds must be charged to my account, not to that of the NAE.

One final word is in order here regarding the book's format. The work was originally proposed with the general reader in view, not the scholar. I have, therefore, omitted an index, included quotations without calling attention to them by indentations, and eliminated footnotes. For the few who may have some interest in my major sources, I have appended a few summary notes at the end of the volume. The book is intended, in short, not as a final word about evangelicalism, but as a conversation opener.

Books are not written without assistants. My benefactors are many. Nearly forty past and present leaders of NAE graciously responded to a modest inventory of NAE's assets and liabilities. This survey is reflected in the last chapter. My thanks go to all of these men even though space did not allow more extensive use of their comments.

Dr. James DeForest Murch, who has contributed so much to NAE, kindly granted me free use of his earlier history of the Association, *Cooperation Without Compromise*. I must also acknowledge my indebtedness to Dr. Clyde Taylor, General Director of NAE, Dr. Jared Gerig, President of Fort Wayne

Bible College, Dr. George L. Ford, Vice President of Azusa Pacific College, Dr. Arthur Climenhaga, formerly Executive Director of NAE, and Mr. Calvin Bulthuis, Editor of William B. Eerdmans Publishing Company, for reading the typescript and offering helpful suggestions for its improvement.

Three of my former students, Miss Carole Swan, Miss Linda Scholz and Mr. Frederick Jarka, assisted me with the research for Chapter 5 and I am grateful to them. A special word of thanks should also go to Miss Marilyn Barrett and Mrs. Doris Lewis, both of whom typed my less than legible copy under unusual pressure of time.

Finally, I would like to thank Mr. Harvey C. Warner, Director of Information for NAE, who encouraged me in this undertaking from the start, and my wife, Mary, who willingly surrendered her '66 vacation in order that her husband might spread his books and papers all over the patio and continue to write and rewrite and rewrite and . . .

—BRUCE SHELLEY

Denver, Colorado
February, 1967

1: What Is Evangelicalism?

On his first Sunday in Georgia in 1735, John Wesley, the young Anglican missionary destined to become the founder of the Methodist Church, sought out a leader of the Moravians, a devout band of Christians working in the colony. En route to Georgia, Wesley's ship had nearly broken to splinters during a storm. The nerves of all on board, including the seamen, had been severely shaken—all, that is, except a group of Moravians. Their peaceableness when the sea split the mainsail and the joy of their singing had deeply impressed the fearful missionary. So Wesley, once in Georgia, made it a point to seek out Spangenberg, the leader of the Moravians, and to ask for advice about his own conduct.

"Do you know yourself?" Spangenberg asked him. "Have you the witness within yourself? Does the Spirit of God bear witness with your spirit that you are a child of God?"

Wesley was startled at such directness and scarcely knew what to say.

His Moravian interrogator noticed his hesitancy and discomfort and so he pressed home an even more personal question. "Do you know Jesus Christ?"

Wesley hedged. "I know He is the Savior of the world."

"True," responded Spangenberg, "but do you know He has saved you?"

Thoroughly at a loss, Wesley stammered feebly, "I hope He has died to save me."

13

But Spangenberg insisted, "Do you know yourself?"

In order to free himself from a most embarrassing situation Wesley convincingly said he did. "But," he later added in admirable honesty, "I fear they were vain words."

That discomforting interview was a landmark in Wesley's pilgrimage toward assurance of salvation. It is also a disclosure of the inner essence of evangelicalism.

From the Philippian jailer who asked his praying prisoners, "Sirs, what must I do to be saved?", to Wesley who squirmed under the heat of Spangenberg's, "Do you know Jesus Christ?", to a teenage terror off the streets of New York who bows in repentance at a Billy Graham Crusade, one major theme runs through that type of Christianity called evangelicalism. That theme is the necessity of personal salvation.

The word "evangelical" is used in our time to designate a group of Protestant churches in Germany, Low Church sympathies in the Church of England, Christians in the Wesleyan tradition, and American fundamentalists. It is most accurately employed, however, in referring to all Christians within Protestant Christianity who emphasize salvation by faith in the atoning death of Jesus Christ through personal conversion, the authority of Scripture, and the importance of preaching in contrast to ritual as a means of saving grace.

Perhaps we can best understand evangelicalism if we consider in this chapter its controlling concepts and in the next two chapters explain how these ideas emerged in the spiritual awakenings of the eighteenth and nineteenth centuries.

In simplest terms an evanglical is a Christian who accepts and lives the gospel, for *evangelion* is merely the Greek word for "good news." In our English Bibles it is often translated "gospel," which is an old Anglo-Saxon word meaning "good (*gōd*) tale (*spell*)." But what is the gospel? It is the blessed bulletin about Jesus Christ (Mark 1:1). It broadcasts that in Him the promises of God, extended to His people in Old Testament times, are fulfilled. In Him the kingdom, the rule of God over men, has come (Matt. 4:23 and 12:28) and through Christ's life, death, and resurrection from the grave all the enemies of man's soul—Satan, sin and death—have been defeated. In His cross rebellious men and holy God are reconciled (II Cor. 5:19); and in His resurrection new life becomes a present possibility for every man (Rom. 4:25).

Evangelicalism, then, begins its explanation of true religion where Jesus began, with "repent and believe the gospel" (Mark 1:15). It emphasizes man's need for a spiritual rebirth in the experience of conversion. Man is not by nature what he must be in order to please God. The change of heart he needs comes only by a creative act of God in response to his deeply meaningful repentance and his living faith in Christ. This emphasis on spiritual rebirth is the genius of evangelicalism.

On one occasion somebody asked George Whitefield, the tireless evangelist of the Methodist revival, "Mr. Whitefield, why do you preach so often on 'Ye must be born again'?"

"Because," replied the great revivalist, fixing his questioner with a solemn gaze, " 'Ye *must* be born again'."

Evangelicals believe that there are two basic types of religion, the interior-personal and the exterior-institutional. They emphasize the first because they are persuaded that the Holy Spirit must do a work in the human heart. Only He can convict of sin and lead the penitent to a renunciation of his sins; and only He can provide the spiritual power necessary to live a transformed life. That is why evangelicals are more concerned about inner personal depth than they are about external churchly conformity.

The spiritual descendants of Wesley and Whitefield differ from many in contemporary Christianity in holding that conversion is a definite, decisive, and profound experience. Without endorsing his total philosophy, evangelicals share the views of Soren Kierkegaard, the nineteenth-century Danish Socrates, when he insists, "As an individual, quite literally as an individual, to relate oneself to God personally is the formula for being a

Christian. . . . If once this occurs, then it is an event incomparably more important than a European war and a war which involves all the corners of the earth, it is a catastrophic event which moves the universe to its profoundest depths. . . . He whose life does not present relative catastrophies of this sort has never, not even in the remotest approximation, had recourse as an individual to God—that is just as impossible as to touch an electrical machine without receiving a shock."

The indispensable means of gaining God's new life, evangelicals are persuaded, is by believing the gospel. Doctrine, then, is important. Evangelicals hold with all orthodox Christians the great cardinal truths of God's revelation. They confess the divine Trinity; they accept Christ's deity and atoning death; they look for a bodily resurrection and a judgment to come; they believe in the church and the necessity of grace. Evangelicalism cannot long survive without orthodox beliefs. Personal faith is in evangelicalism wed to propositional faith. Jesus did not say, "Repent and believe your personal impressions." He preached, "Repent and believe the *gospel!*"

Evangelicals know, however, that the balance between truth as proposition and truth as personal is a delicate one. On the one hand, the loss of spiritual dynamic often jeopardizes basic doctrinal truths. The followers of Wesley agree with Philip Melanchthon, Luther's colleague, when he observes that theology is a matter of the heart as well as the head. Cold hearts, they know, find it hard to embrace the great revealed truths of God's Word. In a lukewarm congregation the surrender of basic truth is so gradual that it is hardly perceptible. First comes a de-emphasis on the value of doctrine. Then, old terms are used with new and equivocal meanings and the naïve are misled. The process can only end in spiritual destruction.

On the other hand, churches sometimes react to a loss of spiritual power by seeking to strengthen their theological positions. As W. Curry Mavis argues, "Theologians then compensate for the loss of inner vitality by rigidly defining doctrinal positions. Theological i's are dotted and doctrinal t's are crossed with a note of ultimate finality. This leads to a doctrinaire situation which is lifeless and empty."

For these reasons, evangelicals, while holding to orthodox beliefs, insist that Christianity is more than theological orthodoxy and religious conservatism. It is a spirit, a concern for sinners, a way of life. Its master motif is the salvation of souls; its guiding image the redemptive gospel of Jesus Christ. All other considerations are subordinated to this standard.

"Orthodoxy, I say, or right opinion," Wesley once said, "is but a slender part of religion at best, and sometimes no part at all. I mean, if a man be a child of God, holy in heart and life, his right opinions are but the smallest part of his religion: if a man be a child of the devil, his right opinions are no part of religion, they cannot be; for he that does the works of the devil has no religion at all." It was this recognition that truth is to be tested by love, that the practical and experiential outcome of belief counts for more than mere soundness of view, which marked the evangelical approach to doctrine.

This pre-eminent concern for experienced Christianity explains why evangelicals have differed with each other over the relation of God's electing choice to man's free will, and yet have found unity in the message of salvation.

In his book *Protestant Thought Before Kant* A. C. McGiffert makes a discerning observation. "It is not surprising," he says, "that the Calvinist Whitefield regarded Wesley's Arminian views as extremely dangerous, and that the two men fell into open and bitter controversy. But it is an interesting commentary upon the gospel's indifference to philosophy and theology that men representing, however crudely and inconsistently, two radically diverse types of thought should both accomplish so tremendous practical results. Ever since the time of Wesley and Whitefield there has been both Arminian and Calvinistic evangelicalism, but the underlying interest of the two types has been essentially the same, and their differences superficial and unimportant, in spite of the large prominence that has been given them."

Not all evangelicals will agree that the differences between Calvinists and Arminians are unimportant, but all will concur that the gospel is the one indispensable particular for Biblical Christianity. Only the gospel, personally received, can convert nominal religion into living faith.

That dimension of depth in faith, which evangelicals seek, has too often been missing in Christendom. The difference between profession of an orthodox creed, evangelicals are persuaded, and the personal experience of Christ is the difference between thumbing through a *National Geographic* and standing on the rim of the Grand Canyon. The church has known her periods of decadent orthodoxy but she has never witnessed a decadent evangelicalism. When the spirit of evangelicalism dies, it ceases to exist.

In harmony with this dominating theme of regeneration evangelicals stress certain other doctrinal motifs. For example, the fall of man. The presupposition of their call to repentance is a realistic view of man.

The great revivalists, as we shall see, whether Calvinistic or Arminian, declared that man was a fallen creature, that he was incurably egocentric, and that he was totally unable to liberate himself from self-love. "We are already bound hand and foot," Wesley preached, "by the chains of our own sins. These. . .are chains of iron and fetters of brass. They are wounds wherewith the world, the flesh and the devil have gashed and mangled us all over. They are diseases that drink up our blood and spirits, that bring us down to the chambers of the grave."

Look, evangelicals cried, at our whirling world! Notice the frustration, the self-centeredness, the barbarity, and the carnality. How can we account for man's own misery and his inhumanity to other men? By one overwhelming fact. He is a sinner, a rebel against God and against society.

This pessimistic view of man's powers explains the popularity of premillennialism among American evangelicals. Beyond man's innate curiosity about the future, the doctrine of premillennialism accents history's frustration apart from divine aid. What every man finds personally—emptiness, futility, and purposelessness—that history without God discloses. Life has no meaning. It begins at no beginning, it ends with no end.

But, evangelicals insist, add God and all is changed. If man transgresses, he must be under law. If he sins, he must have a norm. If he rebels, he must have a Lord. Man cannot now be understood apart from what he once was. Man is made in the image of his creator. His unique freedom granted by God is the presupposition of his misery. Dogs know no guilt; ants dread no death. Only man can sin because only man is made for God.

Conversion, then, the interior turning to God through faith in Jesus Christ, is the clue to the mystery of man. No greater humanitarian labor can be spent than the energy expended in bringing straying sinners to a glorious God.

If the presupposition of the evangelical experience is the sinfulness of man, the means to its achievement is a revelatory Bible. Evangelicalism was brought into being by the Bible; it has sustained itself by the Bible. Unlike scholastic Protestantism, however, evangelicalism, when it has lived up to its own best principles, has not considered the Scriptures as a mere code for conduct or as a series of divine decrees. On the contrary, the Scriptures are life giving because they are life endowed.

One immediate consequence of Whitefield's conversion was the priority he gave to the Word of God. The Bible leaped to life for him. Whereas before it seemed obscure and hard to understand, now it was as clear as the sun at noon. "When God was pleased to shine with power on my soul," he said, "I could no longer be contented to feed on husks or what the swine did eat; the Bible then was my food; there, and there only I took delight." He read the Scripture as it should be read—upon his knees. He endeavored to pray over every line and word. "I got more true knowledge from reading the Book of God in one month," he claimed, "than I could ever have acquired from all the writings of men!"

Wesley reflected a similar reverence for the Scriptures when he wrote: "I want to know one thing—the way to heaven; how to land safe on the happy shore. God Himself has condescended to teach the way; for this very end He came from heaven. He hath written it down in a book. O give me that book! At any price, give me the book of God! I have it: here is knowledge enough for me. Let me be *homo unius libri*."

This instrumental use of the Bible never led the eighteenth-century evangelicals to mere subjectivity. We might suppose that their emphasis upon the Spirit's revealing divine truth as well as imparting moral power would have resulted in the surrender of external authority in religion. But this never happened. Their distrust of man was so great, and their hostility to the rationalism of the age so pervasive, that they took exactly the opposite course. They made more of the authority of the Bible than their predecessors had for a long time before. In opposition to the idea of the sufficiency of human reason, they delighted to belittle it, and to denounce its claims as presumptuous. In resisting it, they appealed, not to the Spirit in the hearts of all believers, as the Quakers did, but to the written and infallible Word. Evangelical influence, and not scholasticism or the Protestantism of the Reformation period, carried the authority of the Scriptures to modern English and American Christians.

It is in this light that fundamentalism can best be understood. Any informed evangelical realizes how often Protestant orthodoxy has degenerated into a rabid sectarianism, and individual fundamentalists have not always avoided this danger. "But if America is not adequately represented by the conduct of some irresponsible tourists," writes Vernon Grounds, president of the Conservative Baptist Seminary, "neither is evangelicalism adequately represented by every snake handler, every holy roller, every bigoted fanatic." Aside from its excess—which every doctrinally oriented movement has difficulty suppressing—

fundamentalism sought a genuinely Biblical witness, a witness for the Bible's unique message of God's redemptive love in Jesus Christ and a witness against the humanized and secularized gospel of liberalism. In this sense, though perhaps only in this sense, fundamentalism was a genuine expression of evangelicalism.

Two predominant consequences have issued from evangelicalism's commitment to a redemptive gospel: first, a controlling and continuing passion to preach the gospel where it has not been heard, and second, a remarkable stimulus to personal and social betterment. Evangelicalism, in short, has greatly furthered missionary activity and Christian ethics.

The story of modern missions is almost exclusively an evangelical saga. From the landing of Pietists, Ziegenbalg and Plütschau, on the beach at Tranquebar in 1706, to William Carey and his colleagues at Serampore, to the host of voluntary societies circling the globe in the nineteenth century, to the Congress on the Church's Worldwide Mission in 1966, evangelicals have shouldered a major share of the heavy burden for a non-Christian world. The achievement of evangelical missionaries between the French Revolution and World War I is nothing less than phenomenal. Kenneth Scott Latourette, the foremost American authority on the expansion of Christianity, has written, "Never had any other set of ideas, religious or secular, been propagated over so wide an area by so many professional agents maintained by the unconstrained donations of so many millions of individuals. . . . For sheer magnitude it has been without parallel in human history."

The motivation behind this surge of foreign mission interest was varied. Unquestionably Biblical imperatives were not always separated from a sense of Western superiority, but genuine scriptural motives more often than not impelled these ambassadors of Christ. Perhaps the dominant impulse was found in the authority of the Bible itself. Had not Jesus commanded His apostles, "Go ye into all the world, and preach the gospel to every creature" (Mark 16:15)?

Wesley, for example, was a man of far horizons. He looked beyond the confines of his little group to the conversion of his native land. He looked beyond the confines of his native land to the winning of a world for Christ. The gospel that was for all must be taken to all, irrespective of color or clime. Early in his ministry he uttered his now celebrated manifesto: "I look upon all the world as my parish; thus far I mean, that in whatever part of it I am, I judge it meet, right and my bounded duty to declare unto all that are willing to hear the glad tidings of salvation."

Another belief that appears time and again in the missionary movement is the conviction that the preaching of the gospel throughout the world is linked to the return of Christ. Many of the early Pietists held the idea that a great conversion of Jews and non-Christians was to be among the signs preceding the coming again of the Lord in glory. Similarly, A. T. Pierson and A. J. Gordon were among the nineteenth-century premillennialists who believed that global evangelization was a prerequisite to the second coming of Christ. They pointed to Jesus Himself who said, "This gospel of the kingdom shall be preached in all the world for a witness unto all nations; and then shall the end come" (Matt. 24:14).

This link between preaching the gospel and the return of Christ was evident in one of the popular hymns of the nineteenth century:

> *Waft, waft, ye winds, his story,*
> *And you, ye waters, roll,*
> *Till, like a sea of glory,*
> *It spreads from pole to pole:*
> *Till o'er our ransomed nature,*
> *The Lamb for sinners slain,*
> *Redeemer, King, Creator,*
> *In bliss returns to reign.*

Joined with this missionary fervor has been the evangelical view of Christian living and morality. Doubtlessly, in evangelicalism the Christian life leans toward the otherworldly. Whether in German Pietism, English evangelicalism, or American fundamentalism one can detect an ascetic tendency. The evangelical ideal calls for a Christian life set constantly upon the future. Natural human interest in the present world is often condemned as irreligious. "Friendship with the world," Wesley said, "is spiritual adultery." This is not to suggest that evangelicals have consistently followed medieval monasticism. They have not, for example, advocated retirement from the world and seclusion in a monastery. But they have denounced many of the ordinary pursuits and pleasures of society, commonly looked upon as indifferent matters. Card-playing, dancing, smoking, horse-racing, theatergoing, elaborate dressing, and frivolity of all kinds have come in for vigorous condemnation. To be a Christian has frequently meant to turn one's back upon "the world."

But this ethic of self-denial was not the result of any delicious morbidity. It was due rather to the conviction that conversion was but the beginning of the Christian life, and salvation to be complete must include the power to overcome sin. That is to say that justification must be followed by sanctification. This, evangelicals believe, is the work of the Holy Spirit in the heart of the believer.

Many of the more vigorous evangelicals felt that genuine faith must be active in love. "A true faith in Christ Jesus will not suffer us to be idle," Whitefield once said. And then in a passage reminiscent of Luther's classic definition of faith, he added, "No: it is an active, lively, restless principle; it fills the heart so that it cannot be easy till it is doing something for Jesus Christ." When this mood merged with the American frontiersman's innate optimism and vigor a whole nation, as we shall see, was energized to repent and reform.

New life in Christ, then, was never intended as a deterrent to social action. The leadership of evangelicals in freeing England of the stigma of slavery and in the scores upon scores of reform movements in nineteenth-century America is abundant evidence that evangelicalism need not be socially sterile.

One of the features of the great missionary movement was the wide variety of humanitarian activities. Evangelical missionaries established schools, built hospitals, trained nurses, reduced complex languages to writing, introduced health measures, taught agricultural techniques, and translated literature into the dialects of the people.

While fundamentalism's reaction to "the social gospel" may be advanced as evidence to the contrary, even there social awareness was not entirely lost. For example, the confession of the Fundamentalist Fellowship of the Northern Baptist Convention affirmed that "human betterment and social improvement" are "inevitable by-products" of the gospel.

No, the testimony from history contradicts the common charge that evangelicalism's morality is solely individualistic. It is true that its ethic begins with a personal redemptive experience of God's grace, but evangelicals have often argued that morality—even social morality—necessarily flows out of a heart touched by divine grace. They knew their Bible well enough to recall that Jesus twice over said of those who profess His name, "You will know them by their fruits" (Matt. 7:16, 20).

2: The Rise of Evangelicalism

The mighty Whitefield, who according to Ben Franklin's estimate could without mechanical means beam his message to 30,000 in the open air, once stood on the courthouse steps in Philadelphia and declared: "Father Abraham, whom have you in Heaven? Any Episcopalians? 'No.' Any Presbyterians? 'No.' Have you any Independents or Seceders? 'No.' Have you any Methodists? 'No, no, no!' Whom have you there? 'We don't know those names here. All who are here are Christians—believers in Christ—men who have been overcome by the blood of the Lamb and the word of his testimony.' Oh, is this the case? Then God help us, God help us all, to forget party names, and to become Christians in deed and in truth."

"Christians in deed and in truth"—that is what evangelicals in every age have sought. Not "party names." Just believers in Christ. Nothing more, but nothing less.

They have surrendered to this single purpose because they believe firmly that Jesus and His apostles were controlled by the same concern. They are convinced that to be a true Christian is to be an evangelical because the Bible makes no distinction between the two.

Unfortunately, during the centuries following the Apostolic Age "Christian" became the label of nearly every individual or group which professed to follow Christ. In fact, the term in-

25

cluded just about everyone in the Western world except the Jews and possibly the distant Muslims. Infant baptism and nominal adherence to Christendom were enough. Saving grace was conceived largely in terms of properly conducted church ceremonies. The gospel, the indispensable element in apostolic Christianity, was all but forgotten.

That is what the Protestant Reformation was all about. When in the sixteenth century Martin Luther, John Calvin, John Knox and the other Reformers attempted to redirect Christianity to the gospel, they received the title "evangelicals" in order to distinguish them from "Catholics." These Reformers, men who hoped to return the true church to the Bible, preached the importance of personal faith as a means of receiving God's righteousness, the direct access of each believer to the forgiving presence of God, and the Scriptures as the only foundation of Christian truth. As a result of their rediscovery of the good news about Jesus Christ, to this day in large sections of Europe and Latin America "evangelical" is used to designate Protestants.

As long as the major Protestant churches accepted, lived, and preached the gospel the title was accurate enough. Unfortunately, however, a century after Luther challenged the Church of Rome with a restatement of the gospel, the Protestant churches, while not denying the gospel, had lost much of its life-giving power. Several of the churches were controlled by the civil government, saving faith was interpreted in terms of mere mental assent to Christian dogmas, and the leaders of the denominations were absorbed in tiresome doctrinal controversies. All this tended to drain off the spiritual vitality of Protestantism.

The recovery of the original Reformation vigor came through a series of movements for spiritual renewal called the Evangelical Awakening. Before the full impact could be assessed, the European continent, England, and her American colonies were dramatically changed. In Germany the movement was called Pietism; in England, Methodism; and in the colonies, the Great

Awakening. Modern evangelicalism is properly traced to this widespread series of spiritual awakenings.

All of the roots of this resurgence are not entirely clear. Historians usually trace evangelicalism to seventeenth-century Holland, where Cocceius (d. 1660), a professor at Leyden, introduced a theology later called Federalism or Cocceianism. Federalism was that refinement of Calvinism which stressed the concept of religious covenants.

Puritanism

However, in the light of the nineteenth-century branches of evangelicalism, especially in the English-speaking world, one of the major roots of this recovery of Biblical Christianity appears to be Puritanism.

Puritanism was a reforming movement within the sixteenth-century Church of England, which in the next century fathered English Presbyterians, Congregationalists, and Baptists. Puritans, drawing first from Lutheranism in Germany and later from continental Calvinism, believed that the English Reformation under Henry VIII (1509-1547) had stopped short of the divine plan for the church.

During Queen Elizabeth's reign (1557-1603) Puritans tried to work within the Church of England and tirelessly attacked what they felt were compromises with what they called "Roman superstitions." They began by decrying clerical garments as unbiblical. It was during this controversy in 1564-66 that they acquired their nickname "Puritan." From clerical clothing they moved on to challenge prayer books and bishops, wedding rings and Christmas observances, lighting of candles and making the sign of the cross. The Puritans wanted nothing less than a reordering of the church according to the Biblical pattern.

When James I (1604-25) came to the English throne, Puritans were driven out of the Anglican Church. They set forth their views before their new king at the Hampton Court Conference (1604), but James made it clear that he would have nothing to do with them. He had seen too much of Presbyterianism in Scotland. He followed up the Conference by depriving 300 Anglican ministers of their livings because of their sympathy with Puritanism.

As a result, open opposition to the crown marked Puritanism for the next half-century. Some of the hardier Puritans sailed for Massachusetts. Others, joining forces with Parliament, succeeded, after a civil war, in toppling the throne in the 1640's. They would at last have their day. The Westminster Assembly of Divines (1643-47) was convened in order to produce truly Biblical beliefs and practices for the English Church. Out of the Assembly came the Westminster Confession of Faith, a classic summation of Reformation teachings—and clear evidence that Puritanism was itself divided. The monarchy was, in time, restored to England and various Puritan denominations were created: Presbyterians, Congregationalists, and Baptists.

The legacy of Puritanism, however, whether in England or in her American colonies, rested in more than denominational groups. It resided also in the spirits of men, in the beliefs of resisters of royal tyranny and in the bravery of pioneers in the New World where the wilderness was to challenge the Puritan's faith—and lose.

For the Puritans, the Anglican appeal to tradition, church authority, and reason clouded the only acceptable basis of life in the church or in the world. The Bible, and the Bible alone, they insisted, was the only safe guide for faith and life.

Two facets of this faith dominated the Puritan mind. First and foremost, the Bible was for them the only way to obtain and experience the knowledge of God. The Bible did not reveal the inmost nature of God. This remained hidden. But incomprehensibility is not unknowability. A faith nourished by the Bible can know that God is in control of the whole universe and that He has chosen some men for salvation from sin.

Second, the Bible disclosed the pattern for ordering the church's life and practice. This belief ignited the fires of controversy with Anglicanism and sparked the different groups within Puritanism itself. Puritans could not agree on what the Biblical constitution of the church was, but all agreed that the Bible, and no other source, contained it.

The God of Scripture, Puritans believed, was the sovereign Lord of nature and history. There were no accidents with God. Providence, God's continual sustaining and ordaining activity in the world, accounted for every single event. Even sin could not be excluded from God's activity, though He was not accountable for it. The guilt for sin was man's, because of the Fall.

Such confidence in God's sovereignty did not, as we might expect, produce a passive people. Unlike scholastic Calvinists who moved from predestination to faith, Puritans grounded predestination in the experience of the believer. And here supremely they proved to be forerunners of later evangelicals. Only the believer, they felt, could say that God's ordination of his salvation was the cause of his faith. Predestination was not a proposition about all men; it was an explanation of the believer's faith.

This faith in God's gracious election implied the responsibility of the elect. If God called them, the Puritans believed, they must live for His glory. Predestination meant that God laid His hand on them for a purpose. In fact, the activity of Christians in the world was a mark of their selection by God. Inactivity was a sign of unbelief. In short, Puritans believed firmly in predestination but it was *experienced* predestination.

The explanation for the balance between God's ordaining and man's maintaining was in the Puritan concept of covenant. The Bible contains the idea of covenant. The Old Testament speaks of a covenant with Abraham, and Jesus Christ introduced "a new covenant in his own blood." A covenant, then, is a compact between God and men. But the Puritans knew that such an agreement could not be between equals. Rather, it was between an initiating God and a responding people. Thus, they sought to preserve both the priority of God and the responsibility of man.

One final tenet of Puritan faith had far-reaching consequences. While the Puritans did not at first question the right of government to order religion, in the course of time they found themselves challenging the monarchy in the name of God. And this was not out of harmony with their belief in God's sovereignty. If Christ is Lord, then no man, whether in state or church, can claim absolute power. Thus Puritanism, though oftentimes unconsciously, challenged tyranny and provided a soil for the outcropping of later democratic societies.

In all these ways, then, in its protest against worldliness, its evangelistic concern, its inward piety, its Scriptural doctrines, its strictness of discipline, the Puritan way of life prepared for the coming of the Wesleys, Whitefield, and all of their train. For good reason John Wesley would later say of Thomas Cartwright, one of the Puritan pioneers, "I look upon him, and the body of Puritans in that age . . . to have been both the most learned and the most pious men that were then in the English nation."

Pietism

With this Puritan background we might expect spiritual renewal to appear first in England. Contrary to expectations, however, the first phase of the Evangelical Awakening arose in Germany in what has come to be called "Pietism." In all Protestant lands the fresh, creative era of the Reformation was followed by a new formalism, but this change was especially noticeable in Germany. The successors of the great Reformers, as is so often true of followers of pioneers, conceived of their task as conservers of the truth won by Luther and his colleagues. Churchmen still accepted the Bible as the source of truth, but they viewed its teaching as collated once and for all time in the theological systems of the Reformation age. This stress on "pure doctrine" produced a new scholasticism, every bit as lifeless as that of the Middle Ages.

Lutheran leaders made much of the church as an institution and of the official aspects of Christianity. Because of church ties with the state, clergymen were treated as the professional Christians. The laymen were expected to attend public worship faithfully, to receive the sacraments, and to assent to orthodox doctrines. This was the sum of Christian experience; this was "dead orthodoxy."

The great reaction to this formal conception of Christianity in Germany was Pietism. The acknowledged founder of the movement was Philipp Jacob Spener (1635-1705). Reared under strong religious beliefs, Spener was later influenced by the German mystic Johann Arndt and translations of the works of the Puritans. After graduation at the University of Strassburg and travels in Switzerland, he became in 1666 chief pastor in the Lutheran city of Frankfort.

Convinced that the religious life of the city was at low tide, Spener, in 1670, gathered a little company of serious-minded men and women in his home twice weekly for devotional study of the Bible. To these meetings the name *Collegia pietatis* (associations of the pious) was soon given. Five years later, Spener published his *Pia desideria* (*Pious Desires*) in which he urges pastors to preach the Word of God to the common man, capable laymen to bear their witness, and all Christians to exercise love, piety, and Christian concern.

In the later years of his life Spener encountered the opposition of the established clergy. For example, in 1695 the theological faculty of Wittenberg charged him with 264 errors, for they recognized in him a threat to the authority of their theological standards. Had not Spener preached that a right feeling in the heart was more important than pure doctrine?

Once underway, however, Pietism was hard to control. Spener was joined in the revival effort by his eminent disciple,

August Hermann Francke (1663-1727), a professor at the University of Halle.

Like Spener, Francke had been hounded from one place to another after his conversion at Lüneburg while writing a sermon on John 20:31: "But these are written that ye might believe that Jesus is the Christ and that believing ye might have life through his name." Halle, however, after 1694, became not only a haven; the newly founded University became the home of Pietism. Francke taught and preached; he built a preparatory school, established an orphanage on faith and answers to prayer, and sponsored the printing and distribution of Bibles. The climax of these ministries came when King Frederick IV, of Denmark, turned to Halle to provide the earliest Protestant missionaries to India. When, on July 5, 1706, the two pioneers, Bartholomew Ziegenbalg and Henry Plütschau, landed on the beach at Tranquebar, a new epoch opened in the spread of the Christian witness.

While most Pietists remained within Lutheranism and gave it, in time, a new character, the movement also nurtured a distinct denomination, Moravianism, which in the eighteenth century was associated with the name of Count Zinzendorf (1700-1760), the passionate lover of Christ.

After the martyrdom of John Huss in 1415 his followers separated into two contending parties. The more moderate group was pacified by Catholic concessions and in 1437 formed the national church of Bohemia. The other group, however, held out for a more radical reform and formed a New Testament community at Kunwald. Here in 1457 they assumed the name *Jednota Bratrska*—the church of the brotherhood. When later joined by other believers in Bohemia, they accepted the title *Unitas Fratrum,* The Unity of the Brethren.

In Bohemia, then, the Brethren worshipped and witnessed until the Thirty Years War (1618-1648) ravaged their land and scattered their families. After the 1620's only a remnant remained in Bohemia to pray for a regathering in God's appointed hour. Eventually that prayer was answered.

Through the good offices of Count Zinzendorf, a Lutheran nobleman who held an important legal position in the court of Saxony, they were enabled to find a new haven. Zinzendorf had felt for some time God's hand upon his life and so had purposed to establish some sort of religious fellowship on a recently purchased estate. When the Moravians, led by Christian David, a convert from Roman Catholicism, made their request to settle in Saxony, Zinzendorf saw God's guidance and gave unhesitating consent. As Christian David struck his carpenter's axe into a tree on the site, he quoted the words of the Psalmist: "Here hath the sparrow found an house, and the swallow a nest for herself, even Thine altars, O Lord of hosts." On June 17, 1722, the task of building began. It was to be a city set on a hill, for the plot of land lay on the Hutberg or Watch Hill. This name, too, was taken as a sign from God. So they christened it Herrnhut—the Lord's Watch. In the next few years it became the gathering-point of the dispersed Brethren, or Moravians as they came to be called after their former homeland in Bohemia.

The Moravians under Zinzendorf's leadership fell heir to the Puritan zeal. In 1732 two Brethren sailed for the West Indies and began a ministry to the Negroes of St. Thomas. The following year a mission was established in Greenland. And in 1735 Wesley was to come under the fire of Spangenberg's questioning in Georgia.

To observers of Christian movements the weaknesses of Pietism are well known. Its emphasis on personal sanctification tended at times to anxious and introspective individualism. Being an exclusive society within the church, it was always in danger of falling into Pharisaism. Because of its concern to rescue individuals "as brands from the burning," it inclined to overlook the lordship of Christ over all men and all of life. This tendency produced in some circles a sentimental Jesuolatry which did less than full justice to the classical Trinitarian faith. Admittedly, then, Pietism, like all other movements in human history, had its weaknesses.

These, however, cannot obscure the necessary corrective it offered to Protestant orthodoxy or the influence it exerted on later evangelicals. It returned the Bible to the common man. It presented Christianity as a living faith, one which begins with a personal conversion experience. And it pioneered the modern miracle of foreign missions. This missionary impulse was created, at least in part, by the Biblical idea that a great conversion of Jews and non-Christians was to be among "the signs of the times" preceding the coming again of Christ in glory, a hope later shared by many of the evangelical missionaries of the nineteenth and twentieth centuries.

Methodism

Perhaps Pietism's greatest contribution to Christian history, however, lies in its influence on Methodism, the second phase of the Evangelical Awakening. Led by George Whitefield (1714-1770), John (1703-1791), and Charles Wesley (1707-1788), the Methodist revival rejuvenated English-speaking Christianity in the eighteenth century and probably helped to spare England from a revolution like that of her neighbor across the English Channel.

Methodism arose in an England which reflected little of the vigorous religious activity of previous generations. The earlier widespread ferment created by Puritanism and the Established Church had all but vanished. The new discoveries of science, of which Sir Isaac Newton's law of gravitation was but one of the most brilliant, were scattering doubts about the older theologies. Men of learning in 1700 viewed the universe as a realm of law. Many of them adopted Deism, a newer system of thought which recognized an all-wise Creator, who, however, does not interfere with His creation. The Deist's God answers no prayers and sends no Savior. Religion, to the Deist, was little more than superstition. It had a certain police value in public, but learned men could afford to repudiate it in private.

The lower classes in England, while unaffected by the ideas of the learned, were in a miserable condition. Drunkenness spread like an epidemic. Jails were cesspools of moral rottenness. Acts of brutality were either ignored or condoned. And the churches, while not without some noble souls, were marked by passionless preaching. Pulpits echoed with essays on moral duties or dreary discourses on intellectual themes.

The revival of emotional utterance based on the gospel of God's grace arose from an obscure student group at Oxford. John Wesley, who had been reared in an Anglican rectory, returned to Oxford in November 1729, to find his brother, Charles, engaged with a few other students in a little club for the nurture of the Christian life. The group soon looked to John as the leader of their activities. They tried to order their lives strictly, to visit prisoners, to fast, to exhort one another, and to partake regularly of the sacraments. In time their earnestness earned them a nickname from their fellow students, "Methodists."

John, however, found little inward assurance from this rigorous discipline. He was still a questing spiritual pilgrim when, in 1735, he sailed for Georgia with Charles. The two years of missionary service in the colony were not happy ones for him but they were important ones. On the voyage across the Atlantic and while in Georgia, he had opportunity to meet Spangenberg and his Moravian brethren and to witness their deep personal piety.

Upon his return to London, John sought out the Moravians and was greatly influenced by one of their leaders, Peter Böhler. He attended their meetings and in one of them at Aldersgate on May 24, 1738, he was converted. While the preface to Luther's commentary on the Epistle to the Romans was being read, Wesley records: "I felt my heart strangely warmed. I felt I did trust in Christ, Christ alone for salvation;

and an assurance was given me that he had taken away my sins, even mine."

After this Wesley might have become another Moravian leader but he could not accept their tendency to withdraw from the world. He was a man of action and fully persuaded that a Christian must enter the world, the arena of spiritual conflict. Consequently, in early 1739, he followed his friend Whitefield into the fields and prisons, preaching the gospel and calling for an immediate and conscious conversion.

England had never before heard two such heralds. They appealed to the heart. They warned of the danger of neglecting Christ. They held before men the forgiving mercy of God in Christ. The preachers encountered ridicule, persecution, and mob violence but they were not silenced. England's hour had come!

The results of Wesley's labor were phenomenal. In a half-century of tireless ministry he rode no less than 250,000 miles on horseback; he preached an average of 500 times annually; he organized Methodist societies; he trained lay preachers; and he added his support to humanitarian causes including Sunday schools, prison reforms, and opposition to slavery. At his death Methodism in Great Britain and the United States numbered 214 circuits, 507 preachers, and 199,735 members. Few men have made a greater spiritual impact upon a nation.

Anglican Evangelicals

As long as the early leaders lived, Methodism remained within the Anglican Church; but after their deaths contrary counsel prevailed, and Methodism became a distinct denomination. In time, however, a number of clergymen within the Anglican Church reproduced the zeal of the Methodists and earned the name "Evangelicals."

Among these, in the later years of the eighteenth century, the most conspicuous figure was John Newton (1725-1807). After a wild youth at sea, Newton was thoroughly converted. Though he was over forty before he was settled in a parish of his own, he exerted, through his exceptional earnestness, an extensive influence on his contemporaries and left to the church a number of heart-warming songs. The widely sung Newton hymn continues to be

> *Amazing grace, how sweet the sound*
> *That saved a wretch like me!*
> *I once was lost, but now am found—*
> *Was blind, but now I see.*

Another influential figure in British evangelicalism was William Wilberforce (1759-1833), who, after turning from a life of frivolity in Switzerland, channeled his new-found faith into action in Parliament, of which he was a member. Wilberforce led the growing forces of evangelicalism in a crusade against deplorable prison conditions, slave trade and other social ills. Success crowned their efforts against slave traffic. In 1807 Parliament outlawed slave trade and in 1833 banned slavery itself throughout the British Empire.

The leadership of Wilberforce and his evangelical successor in Parliament, Lord Shaftesbury (1801-1885), offers abundant refutation of the charge often thrown at evangelicals that their faith is sterile, that it issues in no social action. It was an early maxim with the nineteenth-century evangelicals that everyone to whom the gospel of Jesus Christ had come was bound, according to his opportunities, to impart it to others. To an outstanding degree evangelicals were not disobedient to their vision. They visited the poor, cared for the sick and dying, and educated the unlearned. They poured forth their philanthropies upon the imprisoned, the women and children in the mines, the blind, the paralytic, the deaf and the dumb. From the evangelical impulse came the Church Missionary Society and the Religious Tract Society in 1799 and the British and Foreign Bible Society in 1804. For over a hundred years evangelicalism was a powerful spiritual stimulus within the Anglican Church.

Evangelical Nonconformity

Gospel-empowered living in the nineteenth century was evident outside Anglicanism as well as within. In the first half of the century a new spiritual fervor could be found in nonconformity. The dispossessed of society were reclaimed, the lost children of England were returned from savagery, and houses of worship, once all but vacant, were filled to overflowing with joyful listeners to the gospel message.

Among the nonconformists, the Baptist preacher, Charles Haddon Spurgeon (1834-1892), stood as the embodiment of evangelical belief and practice. He was converted as a teenager in a little Primitive Methodist Chapel and began a short time later to preach with originality and force. He once said that he always preached with the expectation of conversions and in over forty years of ministry he was seldom disappointed.

He was not yet twenty when an old established church, New Park Street Church in London, called him as pastor. The building accommodated 1,200 persons but the congregation which greeted Spurgeon numbered about 80. All that was due to change. Almost immediately the young man's preaching filled the auditorium to overflowing. Two more moves took the congregation to Surrey Music Hall which seated 10,000 people. The rustic youth had entered London quietly but he was not going to leave it as he had found it.

In 1861, the Metropolitan Tabernacle was built. It seated 5,000 people. When the project was launched in 1856 some people called Spurgeon mad, an egoist to think that he could fill it. He did fill it, however, and did so year after year. His preaching was the only attraction. There was no organ, the singing was simple, and the service without designed dignity. But during his ministry 15,000 members were received into membership. Spurgeon used to say that there was not a seat in the Tabernacle but somebody had been converted on it.

From his pulpit issued a number of other ministries of the

gospel. The orphanage, started through the generosity of an elderly lady and often sustained by Spurgeon's own liberality, was evidence of his sympathy for the unfortunate. He also cared for the aged by means of the almshouses for old people. Before elementary education became a responsibility of the state, the great preacher established an evening school in the rooms under the Tabernacle. Open to all free of charge, the classes continued from 1862 to 1899. From the beginning of his ministry in London, his sermons were printed, translated, and distributed around the world. More than 100,000,000 copies of his weekly sermons have been sold. To aid in the distribution of them and other Christian literature the Tabernacle Colportage Association was founded and employed colporteurs who devoted full time to the work. Finally, there was the college, called Spurgeon's College today, for the training of pastors. Established in 1856, it had trained nearly 900 men for the ministry by the time of his death.

One may well ask, "What was the key to his success?" It certainly was not his personal appearance. He was fat and stocky, with an unexpressive face. A popular ballad sung around London when Spurgeon first came to public notice had a refrain, "O my plump, my rosy Spurgeon." His voice, however, was clear as a cymbal and he knew how to use it so as to fill every syllable with meaning. His writings reveal his mastery of the English language. His sermons were the same. Others in his time strove for eloquence; he made it his aim to present the gospel in such a way that it would strike home at once. As one has written: "He substituted naturalness for a false and stilted dignity, passion for precision, plain homely Saxon for highly Latinized English, humor and mother-wit for apathy and sleepiness, glow and life for machinery and death."

One feature, however, above all others contributed to his success with men. He knew God. He did not preach what he had not experienced. Behind all of his sermons was a tremendous force that comes only from conviction and the awareness that he came before men as an ambassador of God. The gospel was for him a converting force or else it was nothing at all. The extent of his commitment can be measured by the fact that money had no attraction for him. After he had been their pastor for twenty-five years, his people gave him 6,476 pounds (about $20,000). He contributed the bulk of it to the almshouses connected with the church. The same thing happened on his fiftieth birthday. It is said he gave away a fortune. When he died he had provided for his widow, but there was little else of which he had to dispose. In many ways Spurgeon illustrates the best in nineteenth-century evangelicalism.

The Great Awakening

The third phase of the Evangelical Awakening arose in the new world. The "Great Awakening" is a term often used to describe the eighteenth-century rebirth of vibrant Christianity in the American colonies. Actually, the "Great Awakening" was a series of awakenings springing from an assortment of causes. The earliest stirrings of new life occurred in the 1720's among the Dutch Reformed in New Jersey and surrounding areas through the fervent preaching of Theodore J. Frelinghuysen. As the Pietists in Germany before him, Frelinghuysen called for a heartfelt conversion. Through the fiery Frelinghuysen, a Presbyterian pastor, Gilbert Tennent, was encouraged to labor for revival among the churches of his area. And thus the revival spread through the middle colonies.

The great center of revival during these years, however, was New England, home of the Puritan theocracy. English Puritans had brought to America their faith in the sovereignty of God, their sense of obedience to the will of God, their doctrine of the helplessness of man apart from grace, and their insistence upon Christian character as the fruit of God's mercy in man's heart. But by the 1720's the vision these hearty souls had brought to America's shores had faded. On the one hand, the shell of orthodoxy lingered but genuine spiritual life had dried up in-side. On the other hand, the spirit of rationalism, represented (at least in the minds of the revivalist preachers) as Arminianism, had entered into the churches. Biblical doctrines were no longer felt; they were merely accepted. Stress lay on the human side of religious life rather than on God's initiating grace. As a result, morality gasped for life and all but died.

The earliest signs of spiritual recovery appeared at Northampton, Massachusetts, through the preaching of Solomon Stoddard and his illustrious grandson and successor, Jonathan Edwards. After distinguished student days at newly founded Yale College, Jonathan Edwards had a conversion experience much like that of John Wesley. As he was reading the Pauline ascription: "Now unto the King eternal, immortal, invisible, the only wise God, be honor and glory forever and ever, Amen" (I Tim. 1:17), there entered his soul "a sense of the glory of the Divine Being." This awareness of the presence and reality of God and of his possible union with his Lord became the guiding star of Edwards' spiritual pilgrimage. A Christian life without an outgoing love toward God and a cheerful submission to all of God's dealings with men was henceforth inconceivable to him. The Calvinistic doctrine which he thus embraced gained its ablest American spokesman, for Edwards must rank as one of this country's greatest minds.

Moving in the light of his glowing conversion experience, Edwards also pioneered the frontier of New England revivalism. When his grandfather died in 1729, Edwards succeeded to the full responsibility of the church at Northampton. Almost at once the church felt the power of his preaching.

In contrast to other revivalists, the intellectual note was heavy but, like Wesley, Edwards appealed to the emotions as well. He set forth in logical power, as well as in vivid imagery, God's sovereign right to deal with men as he chose, the joys of the Christian life, and the fearful terrors of those who persist in their wickedness. Such preaching resulted in unusual conversions, in confession of sin, and in a general improvement in public morality.

Naturally, with his commitment to preaching Edwards welcomed George Whitefield when the greatest of English preachers, in 1740, "touched off a powder-keg" in New England. The torch lit by Edwards at Northampton was carried by Whitefield throughout the colonies. Wherever Whitefield went, men and women wilted in confession of sin before him. The spiritual and emotional explosion from 1740 to 1742 burned the title "Great Awakening" into American history.

Revival fires seldom burn without resistance. The Great Awakening was no exception. The established clergy, especially in New England, voiced opposition to certain practices of the revivalists and certain results of their preaching. The encouraging of lay preaching or "exhorting," the criticisms of some revivalists who charged the established clergymen with "spiritual darkness," the uninhibited "enthusiasm," and the divisions within churches after the revivalists had swept through them—these taken together erected quite a barrier to the continuing spread of the revival.

In Edwards, however, the revival had a vigorous defender. Though not blind to the Awakening's extravagances, Edwards asked, "What is the nature of true religion?" Nothing deserves the name religion that falls short of a remarkable change of disposition, created in the heart by the Holy Spirit, and showing itself in unselfish love for the things of God and in a burning desire for Christian conduct in other men.

With all of its faults, and it had a number, the Great Awakening made its impact upon the American colonies. The movement made a great contribution to education. Princeton, Rutgers, Brown, and Dartmouth were some of the more significant universities created as a result of the awakenings.

Of equal importance was the mood of tolerance that cut across denominational lines. This attitude not only contributed to a national spirit of religious tolerance that helped to make the first amendment of the American Constitution a workable arrangement; it also provided for an evangelical consensus that continues to our own day. Stripped of many European church traditions by the rigors of the American frontier, later evangelicals were inclined to say with Wesley, "If your heart be as my heart, give me your hand."

This, then, the Evangelical Awakening of seventeenth- and eighteenth-century Germany, England and America, is the modern fountainhead of today's evangelicalism.

3: Evangelicalism in America

If the role of evangelicalism on the American frontier could be summed up in an incident, which of course it cannot, one might consider a small event that took place on the outskirts of Columbus, Ohio, in the year 1838. A camp meeting, led by a famous circuit rider named James Gilruth, was in progress. It was night. Lanterns glowed in the darkness—a darkness not confined to Ohio but stretching across most of the continent. A heckler, a muscular ape whose name has long since been forgotten, swaggered through the crowd and began to put out the lights. Preacher Gilruth jumped down off the platform, knocked the ape down three times, dragged him across a creek by the scruff of the neck and flung him, limp, onto the doorstep of the justice of the peace.

Evangelical Christianity faced a rugged test on the frontier but it proved its virility a thousand times over. By prayer and preaching it rolled back the wilderness, built homes, planted fields, educated children, saved souls, and delivered ruffians to the lawman.

Twentieth-century evangelicals in America are the heirs of this rich past. They still reflect a deep respect for revivals as a method for winning the masses to Christ. They continue to employ voluntary societies in obedience to the Great Commission and in search of social reform. And they preach a message and perpetuate denominations shaped out of conflict with the "new theology" of the "gay nineties."

Revivalism

Revivalism was preaching aimed at individuals, confronting them with God's fearful judgment upon their sins of indifference, infidelity, and immorality. Sin and hell were painted in vivid tones, producing fear and dread in the minds of the listener. Then, when the sinner felt the fire of God's impending wrath, the preacher pointed him to the forgiveness of the Lord open to those who repented of their sins and were "born again" by God's Spirit.

While Jonathan Edwards and George Whitefield could on occasion dump sinners into the hands of an angry God, this baptizing in brimstone proved to be the standard formula for spreading the Word of the Lord throughout the sprawling nation. In the nineteenth century, revivalism was not a type of Christianity in America; it was Christianity in America. The century opened with mammoth meetings in the valleys of Kentucky and Tennessee and closed with giant urban campaigns for souls led by Dwight L. Moody. By 1842 Robert Baird, an astute observer of the American scene, noted that revivals had become "a constituent part of the religious system" to such an extent that "he who should oppose himself to revivals, as such, would be regarded by most of our evangelical Christians as *ipso facto,* an enemy to spiritual religion itself."

Nearly every Protestant denomination at some time or other fell under the spell of revivalism's magic, Congregationalists, Presbyterians, Methodists, Disciples, Baptists. In 1854 Philip Schaff, the dean of American church historians, explained to his Berlin brethren that even the German churches in America had adopted the system of revivals and the emphasis upon "subjective, experimental religion." Of all the denominations, however, none surpassed the Methodists and Baptists in their fire and forgiveness preaching. By their ceaseless seeking of lost souls, these two denominations quickly overtook what had once been the strong colonial churches, Congregationalists and Episcopalians. Just before the Civil War the combined strength of Methodists and Baptists accounted for nearly 70 per cent of the total number of Protestant communicants. The search for sinners, animated hymn singing, and "heart-touching" sermons combined to win the West and reclaim the East.

Behind the tents and tree stumps of the revivalist, however, an important though subtle shift in sermons was underway. Formerly the Puritans had emphasized God's covenant—what He had done. This was found in Scripture and in doctrine, and a correct understanding of both was essential. This was taught and made real in the church. But revivalism tended to stress, not so much what God had done, but how man responded.

All "truly gracious affections," Jonathan Edwards had written, "arise from the special and peculiar influences of the Holy Spirit." They are "altogether supernatural." But in the winter of 1834-1835, when Charles Finney was giving a series of revival lectures in New York, he said bluntly, "A revival of religion is not a miracle. There is nothing in religion beyond the ordinary powers of nature." The change could not have been more dramatically disclosed. The Puritan preachers proclaimed God's Word and "waited" for the outpouring of the Spirit. Finney and his followers sought to provoke a revival by using "means."

The triumph of "methodist" revivalism over the earlier Puritan evangelicalism can best be seen in Finney's own revivals, great stirrings of the Spirit which swept central and western New York from 1825 to 1835. A lawyer who had received "a retainer from the Lord Jesus Christ to plead his cause," Finney began his evangelistic activity with the conservative views of his Presbyterian pastor, George W. Gale, but he rapidly moved into the orbit of the New Haven theology of Nathaniel W. Taylor. It is certain that man will sin, Taylor taught, but he still has "power to the contrary." Though man has lost his original righteousness, he retains his free agency. Thus Calvinism, in Taylor's hands, was modified almost beyond recognition on the point of "free will." The revision, many churchmen felt, provided a happy adjustment for their campaign for souls. Finney agreed.

In preaching the sinner's need of repentance Finney was much less subtle than his Congregational and Presbyterian colleagues. He asserted bluntly what many of them were thinking. "There is a sense in which conversion is the work of God," he admitted. But there is also "a sense in which it is the effect of truths" and "a sense in which the preacher does it." The actual turning to God, he explained with an emphasis that suggested that a person saves himself through choice, is the work of the individual. It is what God requires of the individual, and what God requires of him must be something that God cannot do for him. "It must be your voluntary act."

The winsomeness of Finney's ways and the retreat of the traditional Puritan views were evident in his encounter with Lyman Beecher, the organizer of New England awakenings. After an attempt to reconcile the more emotional western preaching with the more traditional eastern type failed, Beecher gave Finney fair warning to keep out of his territory: "Finney, I know your plan, and you know I do; you mean to come into Connecticut and carry a streak of fire to Boston. But if you attempt it, as the Lord liveth, I'll meet you at the State line, and call out all the artillerymen, and fight every inch of the way to Boston, and then I'll fight you there." That was in 1827. Four years later Beecher invited Finney to his Boston pulpit, and admitted that he did very well!

Such conquests were common fare for the fire-eating Finney. He who had seen sinners cut down before him like wheat before the scythe was convinced that God could do almost anything for man and in man. Perfection itself was a live possibility.

Perfectionism

Perfectionism is that view of Christian holiness which holds that the believer through God's grace can achieve and maintain a moral perfection in this life. It nearly always lays stress on a post-conversion experience. The belief appeared in certain utopian sects on the American frontier but it gained widespread acceptance through the Methodists, especially through their extraordinary preacher, Matthew Simpson, and their extraordinary author, Phoebe Palmer, wife of Methodist physician Walter Palmer. So successful were Mrs. Palmer's book *The Way to Holiness* and the Methodist sermons that by 1830 the doctrine needed only the wings of Finney's reputation to carry it across the country. These it soon had.

When Finney moved to Ohio's new Oberlin College in 1835 to take the chair of theology, he made perfectionism a trademark of Oberlin teaching. Though Finney preached and prayed in and out of Puritan churches, his interest in perfectionism was sparked by John Wesley's *Plain Account of Christian Perfection* and his own Bible study. Then in 1843 he underwent a "fresh baptism of the Spirit," a carbon copy of the Methodist "second blessing" or "entire sanctification." This outpouring brought with it a purifying and exhilarating finality which his conversion lacked. From that time, except for a period of illness in 1860, he says, "a religious freedom, a religious buoyancy and delight in God, and in his word, a steadiness of faith, a Christian liberty and overflowing love have been abiding." Like most Methodist holiness preachers, Finney felt that the life of perfection was contrary to luxury, personal adornment, theatergoing, secret societies, and other "worldly" practices.

Once perfectionism could boast of the widely influential Finney, it was an American evangelical current of no little significance. Later holiness groups would look back longingly to the old days when "holiness unto the Lord" was more than a pious

profession. The best loved hymn of the century reveals both the
fervor and the faith which the movement inspired:

> *Rock of Ages, cleft for me,*
> *Let me hide myself in Thee,*
> *Let the water and the blood,*
> *From Thy wounded side which flowed,*
> *Be of sin* the double cure,
> *Save from* wrath *and make me* pure.

Voluntary Societies

The particular vehicle evangelicalism used in carrying forward its heavy burden for America was the voluntary society.
The first English foreign missionary society had come into
existence by an act of Parliament in 1649 in response to John
Eliot's labors among the Massachusetts Indians. In the 1700's
Pietists followed with their missions to Asia and America. It
remained for William Carey, however, in his missionary man-
date, *An Enquiry Into the Obligations of Christians* (1792), to
call for companies of serious-minded Christians to form themselves into societies for the preaching of the gospel to "the
heathen." Once adopted in America, these societies permitted a
quick response to crying needs and mobility in marshalling
support. Various denominational groups could share in the
efforts without raising the troublesome questions surrounding
the nature and mission of the church.

Voluntary societies, then, channeled the energy released by
the revivals into missionary, educational, and reform causes. One
could find in America prior to the Civil War the American
Home Missionary Society, the American Education Society, the
American Temperance Society, the American Tract Society, the
American Peace Society, the American Sunday School Union,
and scores and scores of denominational agencies for dozens
and dozens of causes. Orestes Brownson complained that "matters have come to such a pass, that a peaceable man can hardly
venture to eat or drink, to go to bed or get up, to correct his

children or kiss his wife" without the sanction or direction of some society.

Three factors converged to give the voluntary societies their distinctive character, direction, and force. First, the major Protestant denominations had become increasingly conscious of the ties that bound them together. While denominational labels and even sectarian debates persisted, more and more churchmen viewed the winning of the West, the evangelization of the nation, as a common task. A Parisian pastor who had supposed that the large number of denominations must of necessity "present an obstacle to the progress of the spirit of brotherly love" was astonished at their "harmony and good feeling." "I have understood better, since my visit to the United States," he wrote in 1854, "why our American brethren have shown so little forwardness to unite with us in the Evangelical Alliance. It is because they have its reality at home."

Second, the concern of the churches was not simply to evangelize individuals. It was to remake society as well. They were the heirs of the millennial tradition voiced by Mark Hopkins (1802-87), president of Williams College, when he declared that the time was coming when "wars, and intemperance, and licentiousness, and fraud, and slavery, and all oppression" shall be brought to an end "through the transforming influence of Christianity." While this was to be "the Lord's doing," Christians could help to speed the coming of the perfect society by promoting revivals, establishing churches, and participating in the voluntary societies designed specifically to counter the evils of the times and to promote humanitarian enterprises.

Third, the revival campaigns of the first half of the nineteenth century stressed a doctrine of "disinterested benevolence" as the key to Christian social responsibility. Sin was defined as including selfishness, and the effect of conversion was to shift the believer's controlling interest from self-interest to Christian concern. If one's conversion was genuine, it was insisted, this shift in the preference of the mind would express itself in action.

The conversion experience, therefore, was not the end of the Christian life but only its beginning. Working was quite as necessary as believing, and working meant participating fully in every good cause.

While one can today view this evangelical "piety" as superficial, its achievements, any honest observer must confess, were considerable. The old charge often thrown at evangelicalism, that is, that it is only interested in individual souls and has no social concern, simply will not survive in the glare of historic fact. Whether in the nineteenth-century English Parliament, or on the stumps of America's frontier, evangelicalism was a vigorous instigator of social improvement.

Thanks to revivalism and the voluntary societies these United States were, just prior to the Civil War, "one nation under God." Reporting on the American scene in 1854 to his former colleagues in Berlin, Philip Schaff admitted that "the United States are by far the most religious and Christian country in the world." "Table prayer," he noted, is "almost universal," "daily family worship" is the rule "in religious circles," and church attendance is "inseparable from moral and social respectability."

The New Theology

Though the restless energy of revivalism succeeded in leaving its mark upon American life, certain weaknesses of the movement began to appear in the second half of the nineteenth century. The revivalist faced two temptations. First, he was tempted to reduce "the whole counsel of God" and the complexities of the Christian faith to simple alternatives so that he could call men to a clear-cut decision for Christ. The revivalist well knew that the gospel begins with "repent and believe." What he sometimes forgot was it ends with "teaching them to observe all that I have commanded." Second, the revivalist was tempted to stress results for results' sake and to justify whatever tended to produce them. His message was subtly diluted by his method. As a consequence, revivalists were unwittingly aiding those forces which were eroding American evangelicalism's doctrinal foundations.

Success, of course, nearly always comes with a hidden price tag. The evangelical churches' busyness, their moral idealism, and their increased memberships veiled the cost of neglecting that theological task which is always necessary in order to preserve the true gospel witness, especially in a highly religious culture. As a result, evangelicalism awoke toward the end of the nineteenth century holding its church membership roles while discovering that a new rival was fast capturing the hearts of American Protestants. This new competitor came to be called "The New Theology."

This new way in popular Protestantism held many views in common with later liberalism, but, unlike liberalism, it was a product of the pulpit. Like its sophisticated successor, it was a culture religion, having one basic theological idea. It replaced revivalism's stress on the atonement of Christ by the doctrine of the incarnation, only in this case the incarnation suggested God's presence in the world generally. He was that light of truth in every man which invested human culture with redeeming qualities.

The burst of scientific know-how and industrial expansion which followed the Civil War created an unbridled confidence and complacency among the American people. Opportunities appeared unlimited, and to middle-class America at least, the world appeared rosy red. This tinted optimism was vividly reflected in the New Theology.

In the pulpit of the 1880's Christ was identified with the finest cultural ideals and the noblest human institutions. Any stream of secular thought one might wish to support and any system of values one might choose were readily consecrated in the hands of these high priests of American progress. In this way the New Theology helped to erase any real distinction between the church and the world.

Although the spokesmen of the New Theology clung firmly to the Bible for inspiration and comfort, they considered it a record of the historical experiences out of which the Christian faith had emerged. It was for them a story of suffering and travail which culminated in Christ who walked in perfect communion with God. Its purpose, then, was not dogma but experience, not dead theology but living convictions.

The effect of this new doctrine was to cut the nerve of the evangelistic impulse. If men are naturally religious and if society tends to nurture the natural Christian graces, then the absence of those graces indicates a defect, not in the individual, but in society. Washington Gladden, an effective propagandist for the new views at First Congregational Church in Columbus, Ohio, rejoiced that the "conversion of sinners" was no longer "supposed to be the preacher's main business," and Edward Judson, son of the famous missionary to Burma, declared: "The important thing is not the building up of a church but the Christianization of society."

Henry Ward Beecher, pastor of Plymouth Congregational Church in Brooklyn from 1847 to 1887 and described by Phillips Brooks as "the greatest preacher of America and of our century," may be taken as a conspicuous example of the shift from evangelicalism to the new "liberalism." Beecher stood in the shadow of revivalism. He was a preacher who knew how to get results and his results made him one of the most influential ministers of his day. "I gradually formed a theology by practice," he declared in 1882, "—by trying it on, and the things that really did God's work in the hearts of men I set down as good theology, and the things that did not, whether they were true or not, they were not true to me."

Yet Beecher never ventured to preach about "the passion and death of Christ upon the cross." Christ was an unseen friend, a spiritual presence, a noble example, a king of love, "a man of such purity, wisdom, beneficence, that men believe that he came from above to translate heavenly life and love into earthly conditions," but Christ as truth was subject to individual preferences and feelings, and above all to the pragmatic test of the revivalist.

The evident dangers of the New Theology along with the increasing worldliness of the revivalistic churches caused numbers of believers such travail that several new movements were born. Each of these cried out against the spiritual apathy of the denominations. Out of these voices raised against the drift of the churches, two new forms of evangelicalism were created, each attempting to preserve in its own way the original genius of the movement. The first was a series of churches in the holiness tradition. The second was American fundamentalism. The holiness churches tried to restore Wesleyan piety. The fundamentalists were determined to preserve evangelical doctrine.

The Holiness Tradition

Most of the smaller churches which today perpetuate the Wesleyan doctrine were born out of protest over Methodism's growing worldliness. A number of these were later to find membership in the National Association of Evangelicals.

In 1810 the spectacular evangelist Lorenzo Dow went to England to introduce the camp meeting to the British. Two years after his arrival his converts, professing a return to the perfectionism and evangelism of John Wesley, organized the Primitive Methodist Church.

In 1829 Primitive Methodist missionaries came to the United States, following members who had emigrated to these shores. In this country the church has pursued a democratic polity and, officially at least, adhered to the holiness doctrine of the early English group. Though never large the group has grown steadily, from less than 4,800 members in 1890 to nearly 13,000 in 1964. These are in 90 churches, over half of which are in Pennsylvania.

While Methodism as a whole continued in its quest of holiness after the 1830's, a significant defection occurred in

1843. The Wesleyan Methodist Church left the Methodist Episcopal Church in that year over the abolition controversy, coupled with dissatisfaction over the episcopacy and the state of Methodist piety. The revolting group was made up of abolitionists who agitated for emancipation of the slaves. Their views led them to withdraw in a body from the parent church, taking with them 22 ministers and 6,000 members.

The new group prospered until after the Civil War, when large numbers, considering the main cause of the schism to have been eliminated, returned to the Methodist Episcopal Church. Questions surrounding perfectionist doctrine, however, have preserved the denomination as a separate entity. In 1964 the Wesleyan Methodist Church had just over 1,000 churches and 47,000 members.

After the Civil War the traditionally simple life of Methodists began to change markedly. As the church increased in numbers, wealth, and social status, even more signs of laxity began to appear. As early as 1856 the strict regulations prohibiting the use of certain items of ornamentation in dress were reduced in the *Discipline* to a general admonition. The new freedom was symbolized by Bishop Matthew Simpson's wife, who appeared in ruffled silk, expensive lace, and fine jewelry.

A similar loss of simplicity in worship was evidenced by the costly edifices, choirs, organs, and instrumental music. A correspondent of the *Christian Advocate* reported in 1868 that in the cities of the western states—Ohio, Indiana, Michigan, Wisconsin, Illinois, and Iowa—the tendency was to erect "one hundred thousand dollar churches" where "wealth and style and fashion gather, and the poor have not the gospel preached to them." By the end of the century the grievances were multiplying. Voices were raised against the "church theatricals" and "fairs" that were being held, and opposition mounted against the increasing number of church members who "dance, play cards, attend theaters, [and] absent themselves from revivals."

Evidence of this growing disaffection was apparent in 1860

with the formation of the Free Methodist Church at Pekin, New York. This group was organized when certain advocates of Wesleyan doctrine led by the Rev. B. T. Roberts were "read out" of their churches. The new church took its stance on the declaration that "those who are sanctified wholly" are saved from all inward "sin" and "all their thoughts, words, and actions are governed by pure love." The new group went on to denounce the proud and aspiring, to voice opposition to all "superficial, false, and fashionable" Christians and to demand of church members an affirmative answer to the question: "Will you forever lay aside all superfluous ornaments and adorn yourself in modest apparel. . . , not with broidered hair or gold or pearls or costly array?" Through the years the church has grown. By 1964 it counted over 58,000 members.

The Free Methodist revolt was restricted to three relatively small areas in western New York, Michigan, and Illinois, but in the 1880's evidence of more widespread disaffection found expression in the formation of numerous independent Holiness groups throughout much of rural America. For example, a fourth Methodist group, the Holiness Methodist Church, came into existence in 1900 when certain rural preachers in North Carolina "became intensely interested in local conditions." At a meeting held in Union Chapel Church, Robeson County, these men organized the new body. In 1963 the church counted about 1,000 members.

In addition to these distinctively Methodist bodies other "come-out" groups were composed of believers concerned for holiness from various denominations. One of these was the Church of God (Anderson, Indiana), founded in 1881 with a dual stress on holiness and Christian unity. From its initial base in the rural Midwest, it spread steadily, reaching into the South and into the Pacific coast states. Another group drawing on an intense missionary concern was the Christian and Missionary Alliance, founded by A. B. Simpson, a Presbyterian minister, in 1887. The most successful of these, however, was the Church of the Nazarene, established by a Methodist district superintendent at Los Angeles in 1895 and enlarged by mergers with an eastern Holiness group in 1907 and with one in the South the following year. Drawing dissatisfied Methodists into its fellowship and carrying on an aggressive evangelistic effort, the Church of the Nazarene soared to around 350,000 members by 1966.

Pentecostalism

Experiential Christianity was the concern of another group of churches whose combined membership by the middle of the twentieth century was approximately 1,500,000. These were the "pentecostal" churches. Their distinguishing feature, in addition to the practice of faith healing, was an emphasis upon the baptism of the Holy Spirit, which was manifest by speaking in an unknown tongue.

Modern pentecostalism was first called the Latter Rain Movement, the name being derived from the "former rain" and "latter rain" of Joel 2:23, which was interpreted as a dual prophecy of the speaking in tongues on the first Pentecost (Acts 2:4) and of the descent of the Spirit which was to occur immediately prior to Christ's premillennial return. The movement originated with the preaching of R. G. Spurling and A. J. Tomlinson, an American Bible Society colporteur, in Tennessee and North Carolina at the close of the nineteenth century. Their activity resulted in a bewildering array of Church of God organizations. The largest (over 200,000 members) is generally designated the Church of God (Cleveland, Tennessee), but at least three offshoots bearing the same name have at one time had their headquarters in that small Tennessee town.

Apart from the various Church of God groups whose strength is centered in North Carolina, Georgia, Florida, Tennessee, and Alabama, most of the other pentecostal churches belong to the Pentecostal Fellowship of North America. The largest of these is the Assemblies of God, founded in 1914 at a

convention in Hot Springs, Arkansas. The terminology is somewhat confusing, for the local units of the Assemblies of God are
frequently called full gospel tabernacles or full gospel churches.
The Assemblies of God differ from most other pentecostal
churches in that they regard sanctification as a gradual process
rather than an instantaneous work of grace. Consequently, speaking in tongues is the sign of a second rather than a third
blessing. Though beginning with not more than 6,000 members
in 1914, the Assemblies of God numbered over 550,000 in
1964. Furthermore, they have launched a bold foreign mission program and have witnessed notable successes in many
parts of the world.

The multiplication of these dissenting groups was eloquent
evidence that the once glorious unity among revivalist churches
had tarnished in the air of success and worldliness. Events
following World War I were to make this even more apparent.

Fundamentalism

In June 1922, Harry Emerson Fosdick, the pre-eminent
voice of the American Protestant pulpit, delivered a sermon in
New York's First Presbyterian Church, where he was guest
minister. "The present world situation smells to heaven!" he
proclaimed. "And now, in the presence of colossal problems,
which must be solved in Christ's name and for Christ's sake, the
Fundamentalists propose to drive out from the Christian churches all the consecrated souls who do not agree with their
theory of inspiration. What immeasurable folly!"

Why all this passion in a Presbyterian pulpit? By the second
decade of the twentieth century, Protestants were embroiled in a
bitter theological controversy. The protagonists were the "liberals" or "modernists," who sought to adjust their inherited faith
to the new intellectual climate, and the "fundamentalists," who
insisted that the old ways of stating the faith must be preserved
unchanged. Liberalism drew upon the New Theology of the

nineteenth century—the ties were indeed close—but the two movements can be distinguished. The New Theology reflected the general popular climate of opinion, while liberalism sought to wrestle with the issues being raised in intellectual circles. Fashioned from the pulpit, the New Theology was primarily a preacher's theology. Liberalism was much more a product of the academic concerns of professors in colleges and theological seminaries. Only gradually did it sift down to the American pulpit.

While the terms were often thoughtlessly interchanged in the heated debates, the distinction between "modernism" and "liberalism" depends on whether a system of thought or an attitude of open-mindedness and tolerance is foremost. Modernists were primarily concerned with the reinterpretation of the traditional Christian beliefs so as to make them intelligible in the light of modern scientific and historical knowledge. They preached a gospel of God's Fatherhood. Jesus Christ, who had a unique experience of His Father's fellowship, is, according to modernists, our supreme leader into this communion with God. Like Him, we must recognize the hand of our heavenly Father in all that is about us, in the smiles of infants and in the flight of sparrows. As His children we are all brothers and are therefore obligated to love one another. By introducing into society the moral righteousness that springs from this love, we can expect a bright tomorrow.

It is difficult to discern the limits of the modernist movement because the spokesmen of this trend of thought represented no solid phalanx. At least a half-dozen different solutions to the problem of updating Christianity can be found. The key issue was the authority of the Bible, for Protestantism historically claimed the authority of Scripture for its doctrine and life. Furthermore, it was a highly explosive issue when directly raised, because Protestant piety usually expressed itself in daily Bible-reading as the focal point of family devotions, and thus the deepest emotions of Protestants surrounded the family Bible. The modernist tendency, as exhibited in such men as Shailer Matthews and G. B. Foster, was to reverence the Bible as a treasury of religious devotion but to reject it as in any sense a standard for one's religion. It was suitable for historical study and helpful for devotional purposes, but the test of truth was to be found elsewhere, in the scientific study of men, society, and the natural world.

In back of the modernist's view of the Bible were three nineteenth-century theological tendencies which influenced the liberal and alarmed the conservative. They were (1) the tendency to minimize the distinctions between the natural and the supernatural and to find God immanent in the world, (2) the emphasis on a direct, intuitive experience of God, and (3) the application of the norms of historical criticism to Biblical history within an evolutionary philosophy.

Each of these challenged directly or indirectly the orthodox view of the Bible as the supernaturally revealed Word of God. The minimizing of differences between the natural and the supernatural inevitably suggested that there was no real difference between the Bible and other religious books, thus contesting the whole concept of inspiration. Emphasis on religious intuition diluted the importance of the literal message of Scripture and undercut its authority as an objective standard for human conduct. And finally, the application of evolutionary development to Biblical history directly contradicted the traditional concept of revelation as an objective act of God in history independent of man's moral or spiritual development.

The twentieth-century reaction to these tendencies came to be called "fundamentalism." In 1910 the evangelist Reuben A. Torrey and Amzi C. Dixon, pastor of Moody Church in Chicago, launched an offensive against modernism with the publication of ten small volumes called *The Fundamentals*. Financed by two wealthy oilmen from Los Angeles, these ten booklets were sent "to every pastor, evangelist, missionary, theological student, Sunday school superintendent, Y. M. C. A. and Y. W.

C. A. secretary" whose address could be obtained. Eventually 3,000,000 copies were distributed.

What Torrey, Dixon, and their colleagues hoped to do was to turn the tide of unbelief by establishing five immovable breakers along the shore of orthodox Christianity. In 1895 the Niagara Bible Conference had drafted a statement of five "essential" points of doctrine: the verbal inerrancy of Scripture, the deity and virgin birth of Christ, the substitutionary atonement, the physical resurrection of Christ, and His bodily return to earth. Fundamentalists firmly planted these five doctrines in the swirling currents of theological debate and prepared to resist their removal against every threat.

After World War I fundamentalists carried their campaign to nearly every traditionally evangelical denomination. Among the loosely organized Disciples of Christ, the issues were debated back and forth in the columns of their church papers, the *Christian Century* supporting the liberal position, and the *Christian Standard* upholding the fundamentals. Among Methodists the conservatives attempted unsuccessfully to establish stiff doctrinal standards to which ministers were to subscribe.

Baptists and Presbyterians, however, were the denominations most affected by the controversy. Without any church court system, Baptist fundamentalist leaders organized a Fundamentalist Fellowship in the Northern Baptist Convention in 1920 and sought to gain the acceptance of a confessional statement on the convention floor. After failing in this endeavor many Baptists in the North either created their own Bible schools and seminaries or lent their support to interdenominational agencies. In the thirties and forties three small Baptist bodies emerged from the arena of conflict, the General Association of Regular Baptist Churches in 1932, the Baptist General Conference in 1946, and the Conservative Baptist Association in 1947.

Among Presbyterians, Professor J. Gresham Machen of Princeton Theological Seminary led the conservative resistance to the liberalizing tendencies of the denomination. When Machen refused to surrender his ties with the Independent Board for Presbyterian Foreign Missions, he was brought to trial in the church courts and found guilty of rebellion against his superiors in the church. As a result, the Orthodox Presbyterian Church and later the Bible Presbyterian Church were founded as channels for certain conservative Presbyterians.

Like modernism, the strength of fundamentalism is difficult to assess. The chief reason for this difficulty is the fact that there were many "fundamentalist" churches embraced within the old-line denominations, and the cooperative activities of the fundamentalist movement derive much of their support from members of conventional Baptist, Congregationalist, Methodist, Presbyterian, Quaker, and even Mennonite churches. The Southern Baptist Convention is an example of a major denomination that is staunchly conservative in its doctrinal stance but one not greatly upset by the modernist/fundamentalist debate. The numerical total of fundamentalist denominations, therefore, does not represent the full strength of the movement.

Some index of the magnitude of the fundamentalist mentality was disclosed not long ago in the journal *Christianity Today*. After a 1957 professional survey of the beliefs of American ministers, the magazine reported the following results: 12 per cent of those surveyed identified themselves as liberal, 14 per cent as neo-orthodox, 35 per cent as fundamentalist, and 37 per cent as conservative. The distinction between the fundamentalist and the conservative rested on the acceptance or rejection of Biblical inerrancy.

Sources of Fundamentalism

Such vigor in fundamentalism can be traced to two nineteenth-century sources of conservatism, the Old School Presbyterians headed by Princeton Theological Seminary and the premillennial thought expressed in the Bible conference movement.

When nineteenth-century revivalism swept up many of the old Puritan landmarks, one fortress for orthodoxy remained unshaken. After its founding in 1812 Princeton Seminary provided an intellectual refuge for all Presbyterians and kindred souls seeking solid footing. Princeton theology, as it has come to be called, was founded by Archibald Alexander, given its most complete formulation by Charles Hodge in his *Systematic Theology*, and refined and defended by A. A. Hodge, B. B. Warfield, and J. Gresham Machen.

The cornerstone of Princeton theology was the doctrine of the inspiration of Scripture. The doctrine, the spokesmen argued, had been taught in the Bible and believed in the church from apostolic times to the present. Warfield defined it this way: "The church has always believed her Scriptures to be the book of God, of which God was in such a sense the author that every one of its affirmations of whatever kind is to be esteemed as the utterance of God, of infallible truth and authority."

Supported by a quarry of exegetical stones, the Princeton doctrine of inspiration was erected on three foundational assertions: First, the inspiration of the Scriptures extends to the words of the Bible. The Princeton theologians objected to the suggestion that God used the Biblical writers as robots; they recognized the stylistic differences of the various authors. Their insistence upon verbal inspiration was directed at the effect of the Spirit's activity not His mode.

Second, the Princeton school argued that the Scriptures taught their own inerrancy. As Warfield argued, "A proved error in Scripture contradicts not only our doctrine, but the Scripture claims and, therefore, its inspiration in making those claims."

Third, the inspiration of the Scriptures applies only to "the original autographs." By this the Princeton men meant that the doctrine of inspiration did not safeguard the transmission of the original Biblical documents. Certain copying errors could indeed slip into the text of the Bible.

This case for Biblical inerrancy was widely accepted in fundamentalist circles. Machen carried it with him into his new denomination and into Westminster Theological Seminary founded in 1929. Many others in the blossoming Bible institute movement not connected with Presbyterianism looked to the Princeton professors as their champions. At least three of the articles dealing with inspiration in the *Fundamentals* built their argument from the Princeton doctrine. Even today Warfield's *Inspiration and Authority of the Bible* is required reading in many conservative schools.

The second major source of fundamentalist energy was the premillennial movement of the late nineteenth century. Premillennialism is the form of Christian orthodoxy that anticipates an unparalleled era of peace and righteousness to be established by Christ upon His return to earth. While this belief was widely accepted in the early church prior to Augustine's influential reaction, not until the nineteenth century did the church witness a vigorous revival of the doctrine.

In Europe shortly after the middle of the century two types of premillennialism could be found. Certain prominent Bible commentators, such as Franz Delitzsch, F. L. Godet, and H. E. W. Meyer, taught the so-called historic premillennial position. This view expects a future glorious reign of Christ which will fulfill those divine purposes for the world hidden in the church during the present age. Christ's kingdom, now in the heart of the believer, will then be overt and public. The election of the Jewish people, apparently frustrated at Christ's first coming, will then be consummated though not necessarily by a national restoration. The historic premillennial position, then, affirmed the expectation of Christ's future earthly reign but, following Paul's olive tree analogy in Romans 11, it stressed the continuity of God's redemptive purposes in Israel, in the church, and in the coming kingdom.

The other type of premillennialism received wide acceptance in the Plymouth Brethren movement founded in the 1830's by John Nelson Darby. Through Darby's leadership certain modifications were introduced into premillennialism. The resulting views received the label "dispensationalism."

Dispensationalism, like historic premillennialism, teaches that Christ will return to earth and reign for a thousand years. But it differs from other forms of premillennialism in dividing up sacred history into a number of dispensations or "ages"— usually seven—in each of which God deals with man on a different basis. In the coming kingdom God will deal with Israel once again, for the kingdom will be a national Jewish state. After a period of purgation, called the great tribulation, Israel will, under Christ, fulfill all the Old Testament prophecies of her glory among the nations.

The church, according to dispensationalism, was introduced into the divine order of things after Israel rejected her king, Jesus Christ. The church, then, must be understood in at least two senses. At times the Bible refers to Christendom, which will go from bad to worse in this age until it falls under God's judgment at the end. At other times the Bible speaks of the heavenly people called out of the world and apostate Christendom by the Spirit of God. In Darby's thinking this company made up the Brethren assemblies.

In America the first International Prophecy Conference convened on October 30, 1878, at the Church of the Holy Trinity in New York. The messages of the conference revealed the passion for "the blessed hope" of Christ's return and the prospect of an era of peace and righteousness without associating this hope with any particular scheme of future events.

By the time of the second conference in 1886, however, dispensationalism had found wide acceptance. Men like Nathaniel West, John T. Duffield, and A. J. Gordon continued to ally themselves and their historic premillennial views with Meyer, Delitzsch, Godet, and George Müller, famed orphan leader in England. But the weight of the movement had definitely shifted in favor of dispensationalism. The later publication of the Scofield Reference Bible (1909) popularized even more widely the position.

The popularity of these prophecy and Bible conferences must

be understood, at least in part, as a reaction to the attacks upon the Bible then current. The premillennial views presented at the conferences presupposed the verbal inspiration of Scripture as the basis for the whole system, and consequently the itinerant revivalists who habitually attended the meetings assailed all forms of religious liberalism. The conference speakers identified Christian orthodoxy with Biblical inerrancy, and tested a man's evangelicalism by whether or not he accepted literally the Genesis account of creation, the virgin birth of Jesus, His substitutionary atonement, physical resurrection, and imminent bodily return to earth. The "social gospel" views which many liberals had adopted constituted a double affront to this group because the "social gospel" represented a forthright rejection of their premillennial convictions.

Holding these conflicting views, modernism and fundamentalism were sure to clash. The half-century since Fosdick's fiery sermon, "Shall the Fundamentalists Win?", has not completely extinguished the blaze of controversy. But the light of the flames has revealed a lesson or two. If the theology of the fundamentalists was oversimplified, that of the liberals was oversecularized. If the liberals had a point in insisting that Christianity's survival depended upon its speaking to modern men, fundamentalists were right in demanding that it declare the apostolic message.

As the 1940's approached, then, evangelicals could look back upon their American heritage with a blend of respect and regret. They were the heirs of a zeal for souls fathered by revivalism, a view of ethics weighted toward personal morality, a program of action channeled through voluntary societies, and a commitment to orthodoxy as the only sure word for an unsure age. They were just beginning to look ahead for ways of recovering a sense of oneness in their witness.

4: The Birth of NAE

"We are met here in conference," the Rev. J. Elwin Wright told his listeners at the Hotel Coronado in St. Louis, Missouri, "not to discuss a union of denominations, but to explore the possibilities of resolving misunderstandings, to find common ground upon which we may stand in our fight against evil forces, to provide protective measures against the dictatorship of either government or ecclesiastical combinations in restraint of religious liberty, and to seek ways and means of carrying on for Christ unitedly and aggressively, but with freedom of action within our respective organizations."

Thus Mr. Wright voiced the hopes of 150 delegates assembled for the National Conference for United Action among Evangelicals. The date was April 7, 1942. Today, after a quarter of a century, American evangelicals look to that hour as the birthday of the National Association of Evangelicals. And justifiably so, because two days later a clear pattern for future evangelical endeavor had taken shape.

Four major addresses challenged the delegates to unite in the truth. Dr. Harold John Ockenga, pastor of historic Park Street Church, Boston, Massachusetts, spoke on "The Unvoiced Multitudes"; Dr. William Ward Ayer, pastor of Calvary Baptist Church, New York City, on "Evangelical Christianity"; Dr. Stephen W. Paine, president of Houghton College, on "The

Possibility for United Action"; and Dr. Robert G. Lee, pastor of Bellevue Baptist Church, Memphis, Tennessee, on "Jesus of Nazareth." Stimulated by these men, the conference drafted a tentative constitution and statement of faith, and accepted a report of the policy committee which called for a constitutional convention a year later. At the later meeting official representatives could ratify a permanent constitution and bylaws. The St. Louis delegates, representing some 40 denominations, were clear in their purpose. They were determined "to organize an Association which shall give articulation and united voice to our faith and purpose in Christ Jesus."

The tentative constitution stated that the proposed "National Association of Evangelicals for United Action" was to be purely voluntary and to be operated democratically. The Association was not to conflict with the function, rights, or prerogatives of its members. But membership in the new organization was open only to those denominations, organizations, churches, or groups of churches which could affirm the doctrinal beliefs of the Association and were evangelical in spirit and purpose. The Association would concern itself with (1) evangelism, (2) evangelicals' relation to government, (3) national and local use of radio, (4) public relations, (5) the preservation of separation of church and state, (6) Christian education and (7) the guarantee of freedom for home and foreign missionary endeavor.

Immediately after the St. Louis conference J. Elwin Wright established a temporary office for the Association in Boston, Massachusetts. Regional conferences, held in all parts of the nation, filled the next twelve months. Enthusiastic response to the new venture was everywhere evident. Gospel broadcasting on radio, an issue about which there was much heated controversy, demanded the attention of the new organization. Public interest also ran high concerning evangelism and the separation of church and state. These matters alone demonstrated the value of evangelical cooperation. Evangelicals were convinced that the time had come for the development of a cooperative agency, more powerful numerically and spiritually than any single denomination, for united evangelical action.

As May 1943 and the Constitutional Convention of NAE at Chicago's Lasalle Hotel approached, membership in the new organization increased, expectations deepened, and prayers multiplied. The Call to the Convention stressed the importance of spiritual support: "One thing of greatest importance has not been overlooked and must not be in these next weeks. That one thing needful is earnest, intercessory prayer for a new infilling of the Spirit upon every delegate. Without this, everything that has been done will fall to the ground."

On May 3, 1,000 eager evangelicals converged on the Lasalle Hotel. They Came from some 50 denominations and scores of Christian organizations. After a preliminary session devoted to prayer, the tedious task of building a constitution was undertaken.

At the heart of the planning and discussion at the Convention was the statement of faith. Some pessimists prophesied that the Convention would never be able to agree on a confession of faith. As it turned out, an unusual harmony marked the task. As everyone expected, representatives from so many denominations reflected an assortment of doctrinal beliefs; yet in their acceptance of the deity of Christ and the Bible as the Word of God they were one. All were concerned that the minimal test of fellowship in the Association be explicit on the beliefs that mattered most. They wanted cooperation, but not cooperation which would permit compromise of the evangelical Christian testimony. Without dissent the Convention adopted the following statement:

> 1. We believe the Bible to be the inspired, the only infallible, authoritative word of God.
> 2. We believe that there is one God, eternally existent in three persons, Father, Son, and Holy Ghost.
> 3. We believe in the deity of our Lord Jesus Christ, in His virgin birth, in His sinless life, in His miracles, in His vicarious and atoning death through His shed blood, in His bodily

resurrection, in His ascension to the right hand of the Father, and in His personal return in power and glory.

4. We believe that for the salvation of lost and sinful man regeneration by the Holy Spirit is absolutely essential.

5. We believe in the present ministry of the Holy Spirit by whose indwelling the Christian is enabled to live a godly life.

6. We believe in the resurrection of both the saved and the lost; they that are saved unto the resurrection of life and they that are lost unto the resurrection of damnation.

7. We believe in the spiritual unity of believers in our Lord Jesus Christ.

The Convention then agreed to require members to sign this statement of faith when they joined the Association and annually when they renewed their membership.

The constitution of the Association, once framed, provided that the business of the Association should be conducted by a Board of Administration. This Board included the elected officers of the Association and twenty to forty members at large. The Board, then, was allowed to form an Executive Committee consisting of the officers of the Association and six other members of the Board. This Committee received authority necessary for the proper functioning of the Association. Thus by May 1943 the National Association of Evangelicals was both organized and operating for evangelical interests in the United States.

The Rise of NAE

But how did the desire for a national fellowship of Bible-believing Christians arise? The answer to that question lies in the forerunner of the new association, the New England Fellowship. This New England group was formed in 1929 to encourage evangelical cooperation in various spiritual undertakings. From the beginning, Bible conferences nurtured evangelical unity throughout the area. At Rumney, New Hampshire, a summer assembly drew hundreds of ministers and laymen, as did the camping program for boys and girls and the special conferences for young people.

Soon after its organization the NEF expanded into radio broadcasting. Daily programs over WMEX and a Sunday program over WBZ, Boston, were vital links in the Fellowship's ministry. Thanks to the efforts of NEF, closed churches in New England were also reopened. An extensive Christian education ministry was carried on in the public schools of Maine and Vermont by full-time teachers. And bookstores were established for the sale of evangelical Christian literature in Boston and Worcester, Massachusetts, and in Portland and Bangor, Maine. The New England Fellowship became a signficant religious force in the Northeast where unitarianism, liberalism, and Roman Catholicism were so firmly entrenched.

Under the leadership of J. Elwin Wright the NEF gave birth to the idea of evangelical cooperation on the national level. The NEF conferences in 1939, 1940, and 1941 adopted resolutions calling for the organization of a national fellowship. In the winter of 1940-41 the Rev. Ralph T. Davis, executive secretary of Africa Inland Mission, sent a letter to a number of Christian leaders seeking to determine their interest in evangelical unity especially in missionary endeavor. Many of these responses were encouraging. NEF's Dr. Wright followed this by a tour of 31 states in 1941, interviewing personally many evangelical leaders. As a result, on October 27 and 28 of that year several men who had manifested an unusual interest in greater cooperation met at Moody Bible Institute in Chicago for discussion and a time of prayer.

At the meeting the group unanimously decided that the next step should be a call for a national conference of evangelicals, including leaders of various denominations, mission boards, colleges, seminaries, Bible institutes, the religious press, and interdenominational organizations. This Chicago group felt that such a later gathering could receive and consider all suggestions and plans for evangelical action, including those of the recently formed American Council of Christian Churches. This, then, was the immediate stimulus to the National Association of Evangelicals.

The character of the National Association of Evangelicals, however, was shaped by three deeper roots. As the official Call to the St. Louis conference expressed it: "Membership will be on a basis of the traditionally accepted evangelical position." That position encompassed three nineteenth-century concepts: (1) the associational idea among evangelicals, (2) the denominational view of the church, and (3) the concept of voluntary societies as means of advancing the Christian witness.

The Idea of an Association

Out of the fervent missionary spirit of nineteenth-century evangelicalism a number of powerful appeals for federation issued. For example, Samuel S. Schmucker (1799-1873), a Lutheran professor of theology at the Theological Seminary at Gettysburg, published in 1838 his *Fraternal Appeal to the American Churches.* In 1845, he released his *Overture for Christian Union* and a composite *United Protestant Confession,* which was drawn from the credal statements of various churches and indicates a commonly accepted core of belief among Protestants in 1845. The *Appeal* and *Overture* aroused much discussion and might well have led to an ecumenical group in America, but in 1846 evangelicals from the United States and representatives from around the world were called to meet in London to organize an evangelical alliance. Schmucker and other American evangelicals abandoned their own plans in order to join this new expression of evangelical unity.

Sparked by the leadership of the great Scottish preacher, Thomas Chalmers, a preliminary gathering of the Evangelical Alliance met at Liverpool in 1845. It was from this conference that the invitations were issued to Protestants around the world to come to London in August 1846 for united counsel and action. In response to the invitations, over 800 churchmen gathered in Freemason's Hall and unanimously adopted a resolution. "The members of this conference," it said, "are deeply convinced of the desirableness of forming a confederation, on the basis of great Evangelical principles held in common by them which may afford opportunity to the members of the Church of Christ of cultivating brotherly love, enjoying Christian intercourse, and promoting such other objects as they may hereafter agree to prosecute together; and they hereby proceed to form such a Confederation under the name of The Evangelical Alliance."

The conference also accepted a statement of principles essential to cooperation. The statement included testimony to the divine inspiration of the Scriptures, the Holy Trinity, the utter depravity of human nature, the incarnation of the Son of God, His atonement for the sins of mankind and His mediatorial intercession, the justification of the sinner by faith alone, and the work of the Holy Spirit in conversion and sanctification of the sinner.

While the extent of the statement and some of its phrasings were not pleasing to the Americans, they accepted them in principle and came home eager to set up a national Alliance. The threatening clouds of the Civil War, however, hindered all such attempts. Not until 1867 did the American phase of the work begin. Mr. William E. Dodge, a prominent and philanthropic businessman from New York City, was chosen president and held the office for sixteen years. In 1873 the international conference convened in America, the most notable of a series of world gatherings of the Alliance. A full-time American general secretary, Dr. Josiah Strong, was employed in 1886 and the Alliance gained wider and wider support.

Although the Evangelical Alliance was composed only of interested individuals and had no official connections with organized churches, it was a sounding board for many opinions and gave its members a vision of what could be done. One of the American leaders of the Alliance, Dr. Philip Schaff, the noted church historian, told a Chicago gathering in 1893 that the Alliance offered the hope of the reunion of Christendom.

The Alliance defended religious liberty wherever it was threatened and became a powerful advocate of missions. Its journal, *Evangelical Christendom*, was the Ecumenical Press Service of its day, and its worldwide annual week of prayer enlisted the participation of 50,000 churches. In short, it succeeded in breaking down walls of denominational bigotry and in giving Protestantism a new vision of "one body in Christ."

Unfortunately, American involvement in the Alliance was never wholehearted. When the Branch on this side of the Atlantic was organized in 1867 the leaders felt it necessary to add a qualifying preamble to the articles of faith. And even in the heyday of the Alliance in the United States, rumblings of discontent were sounding. Dr. Strong was one of the leaders in the "social gospel" movement and urged that the churches cooperate in helping to Christianize the social order and in bringing the kingdom of God to earth. In 1898 he resigned as secretary of the American branch to take an active part in the organization of the Federal Council of Churches of Christ in America (1908).

The Federal Council sought a federated union not of individuals but of churches, an advisory group rather than an organic union, "with no authority to draw up a common creed or form of government or of worship or in any way to limit the full autonomy of the Christian bodies adhering to it." It was formally organized in 1908 and embraced 31 of the major American denominations.

The Council's preamble and plan of federation (1908), as well as "The Social Creed of the Churches" issued in 1912, revealed clearly the spirit of the liberal social gospel. The plan of federation declared that the object of the Council was "to secure a larger combined influence for the churches of Christ in all matters affecting the moral and social condition of the people, so as to promote the application of the law of Christ in every relation of human life."

By 1950 the Federal Council represented 144,000 local congregations and a total membership of 32,000,000. In that year the Council merged with a number of other interdenominational agencies in the United States to form the National Council of the Churches of Christ in the United States of America. The National Council represented an enlargement of the Federal Council in order to consolidate various agencies and tasks. Its aims, however, remain virtually the same as those of its predecessor. Like the Federal Council it attempts to speak as "the conscience of Protestantism" on issues embracing almost every branch of Christian living.

With the rise first of the Federal Council and later the National Council the death of the American branch of the Evangelical Alliance was all but assured. Its own internal weaknesses left it inadequately prepared to face the challenges of the twentieth century.

Fortunately, the British organization, the oldest and largest of the various national bodies, was more firmly committed to a distinctively evangelical witness. Even though its influence declined in the twentieth century, it continued to promote a limited spiritual ministry until, joined by the National Association of Evangelicals, it gave birth in 1951 to the World Evangelical Fellowship, an international body committed to the evangelical testimony.

The Denominational Concept

The second nineteenth-century root of the flowering NAE was the denominational concept of the church. This idea of denominations first arose among a group of English Puritans called Independents. These men, some of them constituting the minority voice in the Westminster Assembly (1643), were much like later Congregationalists. In their minds the word "denomination" implied that a particular body of Christians (let us say, for example, the Baptists) was only a portion of the total Christian Church, called or denominated by its particular name, "Baptist."

Central to this idea was the conviction that no single body of beliefs can ever fully represent the total claim of God upon the minds and hearts of men. In fact, so these Independents argued, God has His hand in the divisions within Christianity to bring forth more light. "Sparks," they said, "are beaten out by the flints striking together. Many sparks of light, many truths, are beaten out by the beatings of men's spirits one against another."

Prior to the nineteenth century, various groups justified their separation from other Christians by this line of reasoning. In America, however, where the revivalist mood belittled traditional church doctrine and order and stressed instead the importance of the internal work of the Spirit of God, this view triumphed over every foe.

Drawing satisfaction from the wellspring of denominational theory, the Rev. Albert Barnes, the distinguished Presbyterian minister and Bible commentator, declared in 1840, "The spirit of this land is, that the Church of Christ is not under the Episcopal form, or the Baptist, the Methodist, the Presbyterian, or the Congregational form exclusively; all are, to all intents and purposes, to be recognized as parts of the one holy catholic church." Most nineteenth-century evangelicals, at least before the Civil War, would have agreed with Barnes. The "visible church," they felt, included denominations, voluntary societies, and local congregations.

In the twentieth century, however, another mood stirred among the churches. Immigrations in the second half of the nineteenth century brought millions of Roman Catholics, Lutherans, and members of other European religious groups to American shores. Most of the churchmen from these denominations, rooted as they were in a deep tradition of churchmanship, shared neither the revivalistic mentality of American evangelicalism nor its concept of the universal church. They considered revivals "pietistic" and disruptive.

Moreover, the growing tide of ecumenical interest in the twentieth century swept up some weather-beaten and tattered criticisms of denominationalism. "Unhappy divisions," "the scandal of divided Christendom," "the perverse spirit of sectarianism," and other such charges surged up against the traditional attitude of American Protestantism. As a result of this mood, several major mergers of denominations were completed in the first half of our century.

The groups joining NAE had not encouraged either of these developments, and for that reason they reflected more of Barnes' nineteenth-century attitude toward denominations. They did not consider denominations sinful. Nor did they view separate groups in and of themselves destructive of Christian unity. Christian unity after all rested less in ecclesiastical conformity than in personal spirituality. It was less a matter of external forms than of internal faith.

The Voluntary Society

The third nineteenth-century root supplying to NAE a certain character was the voluntary society. As we have seen, these interdenominational organizations served American revivalistic, missionary, and educational purposes well. Without raising troublesome questions about the Biblical bases of cooperation or about the implied concept of the church, they had helped to spread the knowledge of the Lord throughout the nation.

In the twentieth century, however, the character of Protestant cooperation shifted. The denominations themselves instigated this shift by taking over many of the responsibilities formerly discharged through the interdenominational voluntary societies. The Christian Endeavor societies, for example, had been displaced in most of the churches by denominational "youth fellowships." The Student Christian Movement was largely replaced by denominational student groups. The Sunday school interest was diverted into denominational channels with denominational lesson materials assiduously and profitably promoted.

Thus, when in the 1920's the fundamentalists lost the struggle for control of the denominations, they had no recourse. They turned to the existing interdenominational agencies and created still others in order to fulfill their educational, missionary, and social service ministries.

In this way, fundamentalist and evangelical groups fell heir to the voluntary society pattern of cooperation. Youth for Christ, the Inter-Varsity Christian Fellowship, the Christian Business Men's Committee, and scores of other organizations followed the earlier plan. Thus, when the National Association of Evangelicals was organized, it helped to link some three or four million "fundamentalists" for purposes of cooperative action in one great voluntary society with membership available to individuals, local churches, and a variety of other organizations.

Reasons for NAE

It would be impossible to enumerate here all the reasons for the creation of NAE. No one really knows all the motives. Three major reasons, however, appeared from time to time in the correspondence and in the public messages of the St. Louis conference.

Chief of these was undoubtedly a dissatisfaction with other expressions of Christian unity. The Federal Council of Churches of Christ had from its inception proved too liberal, especially in its "social gospel," to gain widespread evangelical support. Most conservatives felt that the Council ignored the only sure Christian basis of social change, the necessity of personal conversion and the regenerated life.

The Federal Council of Churches was undoubtedly in view when the St. Louis conference's resolution declared: "We realize that in many areas of Christian endeavor the organizations which now purport to be the representatives of Protestant Christianity have departed from the faith of Jesus Christ. We do now reaffirm our unqualified loyalty to this Gospel as herein set forth, declaring our unwillingness to be represented by organizations which do not have such loyalty to the Gospel of Christ."

On the other hand, the vast majority of the founders of NAE were not interested in a unity based on criticism. They regarded the position of the Rev. Carl McIntire and his recently created American Council of Christian Churches unacceptable. During the October (1941) meeting of evangelical leaders at Moody Bible Institute, the purpose, organization, and program of the then month-old ACCC were presented, but the evangelicals there assembled did not feel that the ACCC would properly express the ideals they shared for a positive evangelical witness.

At the St. Louis conference Mr. McIntire was twice granted opportunity to present the work of ACCC, but again the delegates voted to proceed with the creation of NAE for its own distinctive purposes as outlined in the conference Call.

Dr. Stephen Paine in his address, "The Possibility for United Action," warned of the dangers of unity founded on negation. "Let us remember," he said, "that negative motives often unite factions which otherwise could never work together. But remember also that these negative motives for united action contain within themselves the very seeds of disintegration. They are *centrifugal,* and as soon as the immediate pressure is lessened, the supposed unity of action flies to the four points of the compass."

Since, then, other organizations failed to meet the need, these evangelical leaders felt that a new channel of endeavor was the only alternative.

Akin to this motive was a second, a sense of isolation among conservative Christians. Dr. Harold John Ockenga spoke of this in his message at St. Louis, "The Unvoiced Multitudes." "I, myself, am one of the unvoiced multitude," he said. "I represent Mr. John Q. of the clergy, or, if you please, one of the unrepresented preachers in the concerted movements of our day. You may be sure that I keenly feel this position of a lone wolf, as I have sometimes been called, but I recognize that there are many lone wolves in the ministry today who in a measure have been greatly blessed by God in their own particular fields of endeavor. Yet I see on the horizon ominous clouds of battle which spell annihilation unless we are willing to run in a pack."

Doubtless, the fragmentization of Christian ranks as a result of the fundamentalist-modernist controversy had reached a point of necessary reaction. Zeal for truth had too often trampled Christian unity underfoot.

Dr. Ockenga stressed this when he told the St. Louis assembly, "This millstone of rugged independency which has held back innumerable movements before, in which individual leaders must be the whole hog or none, must be utterly repudiated by every one of us. A terrible indictment may be laid against fundamentalism because of its failures, divisions, and controversies. This must be admitted by those of us who believe in the fundamentals and who also seek a new outlook."

The third motive for the creation of NAE was the firm conviction that a positive witness could be given by united evangelicals and only by united evangelicals. The Call to the St. Louis conference declared: "It is our belief that something of this nature can become a basis for an effective cooperation among evangelicals by which our mutual interests may be conserved and aided. There are millions of evangelical Christians in this country who feel that at present they have no corporate means of making their wishes known in matters common to all. We believe the time has come to render God this service."

During the sessions of the conference Dr. Ockenga once again voiced the persuasion of many when he asserted, "If we are to guard our testimony and our purity, our great need is not for something which is negative but something which is positive, something which will launch a program, something which will marshal the enthusiasm and the resources and the strength of the people of Christian conviction throughout America. I am convinced that if that positive attitude is taken, the clear, concise, definite view, we shall receive the response which is necessary. God will add His blessing in a marvelous way."

These, then, were at least three of the reasons for NAE in 1942: the inadequacy of other channels of cooperation, the sense of isolation felt by many conservative Christians and organizations, and the conviction that a united evangelical testimony would honor God.

Only some such cluster of incentives could explain the times of prayer during those early months and how representatives from 40 denominations could find so little difficulty in arriving at the basic doctrinal agreement reached at St. Louis. Many evangelicals were convinced that the time had come for united action on the national level.

5: NAE:
Ministry and Maturity

A bewildered look crept across the sales manager's face as he stepped from the hotel elevator. "Evangelical Teacher Training Association, Campus Crusade, Audio Visual Library," he read as his curiosity propelled him down the row of displays. Apart from the titles, it all seemed like the state fair booths he used to visit as a boy, or like a score of conventions he had attended for his company.

"What sort of outfit is this?" he asked himself. He glanced into a conference room where an open door revealed middle-aged men around a table, engaged in vigorous discussion. No familiar smoke gushed through the doorway, but other than that it could have been a sales meeting of Union Carbide representatives or a committee of the local American Cancer Society.

"What goes here?" he finally asked a clerk at the registration desk. "This?" responded the surprised lady. "Why, this is the convention of the National Association of Evangelicals."

In the conference rooms and on the convention floor something significant has been happening within American evangelicalism. NAE has been extending its ministry and gaining a new maturity.

Twenty-five years have now ebbed into yesterdays since the birthday of NAE (April 7, 1942) at the Hotel Coronado in St.

Louis. Today, after a quarter of a century, what can the Association point to with a sense of achievement? How have the intervening years vindicated the vision of those concerned evangelicals who gathered in 1942?

Perhaps the greatest accomplishment of NAE is the fact of its continuing existence. Leaping over denominational walls the Association, through its statement of faith, now provides evangelical identification for 29,000 churches and 2,500,000 Christians. Through its affiliated agencies it offers a channel of cooperation over which a united evangelical witness can be beamed for several million more. The Board of Administration, composed of representatives from constituent denominations and some members elected at large, is itself a reflection of this evangelical ecumenicity, as it coordinates the ministries of the various commissions and affiliated organizations.

The maintenance of contact with the assorted agencies and the oversight of the various facets and functions of the Association fall to NAE's General Director, Dr. Clyde Taylor. No man over the past twenty-five years has contributed more to American evangelical cooperation than has Clyde Taylor. His role as General Director is a recent one, but prior to that he served as head of the Office of Public Affairs for the NAE and as Executive Secretary for the Evangelical Foreign Missions Association, two posts he continues to fill. Someone who knew the work of NAE well called Clyde Taylor, "Mr. NAE." He was not far from the truth.

The headquarters for the Association, located in Wheaton, Illinois, is, however, a beehive of activity in its own right. The Executive Director there is directly responsible for the field services of the NAE, including its regional offices; the office of information which publishes *United Evangelical Action;* and the implementation of the Association's programs. *Action* magazine is now edited by the Director of NAE's Information Office, Mr. Harvey Warner.

The Public Affairs Office in Washington, D. C., performs a

strategic service for evangelicals. It keeps the churches informed of the actions of the various branches of government and represents evangelicals to the government on matters of particular interest to conservative Christians such as infringements of religious liberty, the role of the military chaplains, and missionary problems overseas.

The united evangelical character of the NAE is reflected not only in its administration but also in the ministries of the various commissions and affiliated organizations. Unfortunately, it is impossible within the limits of this chapter to treat every activity of the Association. It seems best therefore to take note of the central concerns of NAE: evangelism, Christian nurture, missions and social action—all historic interests of evangelicals.

Evangelism

The very name of the Association—the National Association of *Evangelicals*—implies a deep commitment to *evangelism*. Through the years the integrating thread of the cooperative efforts of evangelicals has been the objective to make the saving message of Christ known. Back in 1957 *United Evangelical Action* reflected, "Evangelism quietly, but powerfully, flows through many channels of the National Association of Evangelicals' endeavor. . . . In their respective fields of service many of the agencies and commissions of the NAE further the cause of evangelism." This commitment to the preaching of God's mercy in Christ, James DeForest Murch concluded, was one major reason for the forward thrust of the Association and the unity of believers in the NAE.

A mere listing of commissions and affiliate organizations will support the editor's contention that evangelism is one of the mainsprings of the Association. The Commission for Evangelism and Spiritual Life, the Commission for Church Extension and Home Missions, and the National Religious Broadcasters are each in their own way centrally occupied with making Christ known.

When the Commission on Evangelism was created in 1942, it immediately gave enthusiastic support to evangelism. Evangelists Bob Jones, Sr., John R. Rice, Hyman Appelman, Charles E. Fuller, Walter A. Maier, and other nationally known speakers were encouraged in their efforts to turn men to Christ. At the same time, during the years of World War II, many evangelicals felt a spiritual obligation for American youth. As preachers saw young people responding to the gospel, it was evident that a concerted effort to reach even more was necessary. Youth for Christ sprang into being in order to rally evangelical churches to the need of evangelism for teens. Sizeable auditoriums across the country were soon filled on Saturday nights with teenagers. Decisions for Christ followed.

The Commission on Evangelism in the meantime continued to encourage unified evangelistic campaigns with the support of member churches of the NAE. In 1945, Melville G. Hatcher was appointed the Association's first Secretary of Evangelism. Under Hatcher's direction the work of the commission continued to expand until 1950, when the whole question of evangelism and the churches arose as a major concern of the Indianapolis Convention.

Several of the denominations objected to NAE's sponsorship of evangelistic campaigns. Consequently, the Indianapolis Convention passed a resolution calling for the continuation of the Association's encouragement of evangelism but the return of all direction of campaigns to the hands of the churches. The Commission on Evangelism was allotted three distinct areas of work: encouragement of regional conferences, organization of study groups to help united effort, and publication of evangelistic aids.

After adopting these modifications the Commission on Evangelism continued to stimulate evangelistic efforts and to support revivalists such as Billy Graham. A number of evangelists were invited and crusades organized by NAE member churches. Reflecting upon these efforts, James DeForest Murch in a

United Evangelical Action editorial in 1958 wrote, "Where would the cause of evangelical Protestantism in America be today if the N.A.E. had not been born? In evangelism, Billy Graham and other evangelical evangelists have had its unwithholding cooperation, its constituency has been the faith and prayer nucleus around which community wide support has been built."

But other problems were also facing the churches in the 1950's. That was the big decade in suburban developments. Suburban and city planning committees were inadvertently bypassing the smaller evangelical denominations when plans were projected for new housing areas. According to the American Institute of Planners, the principle of comity had to be observed. Only one church would be allowed to build a structure in a neighborhood of a specified number of people. If the number was doubled, then two churches could be erected.

Evangelicals were aroused when it became apparent that the National Council of Churches was the sole spokesman for Protestant churches. The NAE through its Executive Director, Dr. George L. Ford, protested this policy and as a result the Commission on Church Extension gained recognition from the Institute.

Crises of this sort, however, were commonplace. Continual alertness for possible comity discrimination in any part of the country rested on the shoulders of the Commission on Church Extension and those of NAE area representatives. The value of this watchfulness was illustrated in 1958 when a church in Washington, D.C., was told by the Redevelopment Land Agency which was clearing the area where the church was located that it didn't stand "a ghost of a chance" of securing a location in the redeveloped community unless it cooperated with the Washington Council of Churches. The NAE was able to point out the illegality of this approach to the Redevelopment Land Agency and to obtain promises that the church would not be discriminated against because it had religious convictions against cooperating with the Council of Churches.

The Church Extension Commission, however, is more than a watchdog of community planning and redevelopment. In recent years it has supplied the churches with information regarding population shifts and matters of national census; it has sought to bridge the gap between the churches and evangelical educational endeavor touching urban problems; and it has provided inspiration for evangelism and home missions. From time to time the Commissions on Evangelism and Church Extension have also stimulated visitation seminars, laymen's leadership institutes, the ministry of industrial chaplains, and, in the last five years, the awareness of the crying needs of the inner city.

Over the years the Spiritual Life Commission also has made a significant contribution to the renewal of the churches. For example, the Commission has through the years published a worship booklet designed for use on the World Day of Prayer. The booklet contains suggested Scripture passages, hymns, and other related elements of worship. The outstanding feature is its emphasis on Christian spiritual unity. Evangelicals, the Commission believes, can contribute to a truly Biblical ecumenicity.

Thanks to the Spiritual Life Commission's efforts, many communities in the United States have witnessed the unifying influence of the Holy Spirit as Christians from various denominations have joined in prayer for revival. United Easter sunrise services have assumed greater meaning and Thanksgiving Day gatherings have reflected the reality of Christian unity.

The story of NAE's contribution to the freedom of religious radio broadcasting is one of the significant chapters in the twenty-five year history of the Association. The demand for united evangelical action regarding broadcasting was one of the earliest cries for NAE's leadership. Radio stations in 1943 were feeling the pressure to accept none other than broadcasts authorized by the Federal Council of Christian Churches. Charges of "radio racketeering" and "independent superfundamentalist revivalists" had been circulating for some time. To correct the supposed abuse of the air waves, the Federal Council advanced its own claims to the guardianship of Protestant broadcasting and persuaded the Mutual Broadcasting System to allocate time only to the three major religious groups in the United States, Protestants (FCC), Catholics, and Jews. Late in 1943 it appeared that the Council had reached its goal.

Shortly after its organization in 1943, however, the National Association of Evangelicals began a study of the use of radio time. Some index of the deep involvement of conservatives in broadcasting was given by *Christian Life* magazine in 1948 when it indicated fundamentalists were sponsoring 1,600 programs each week. Quite naturally, then, the NAE was concerned with a plan of protection for the rights of evangelical broadcasters in the area of preaching doctrinal sermons, the purchase of radio time, and the right of evangelicals to their share of the sustaining (free) time allotted to Protestantism. In April 1944, at the invitation of the NAE, 150 evangelical broadcasters assembled in Columbus, Ohio, where the second annual convention of the NAE was in session. The purpose of the meeting was to form a national association of gospel broadcasters to be affiliated with the NAE.

By September 1944, the religious broadcasters were able to hold their constitutional convention in Moody Memorial Church in Chicago. Officers for the National Religious Broadcasters were chosen and, in order to maintain the highest standards of broadcasting, a code was adopted and was signed by each member of the NRB. It sought to safeguard responsible evangelicals from religious racketeers on the one hand and ecclesiastical boycotters on the other. It called for programs sponsored solely by non-profit organizations, for "positive, concise and constructive" messages, cooperation with stations and network managements, and businesslike financial practices.

In subsequent years the code of ethics, the NRB Constitution and Bylaws, and a copy of a 1946 resolution explaining the differences between evangelicals and other self-appointed spokesmen for American Protestantism were sent to all radio networks and local station managers in the hopes that the radio stations would accept and respond favorably to a request for radio time. The plan succeeded. Through the efforts of the National Religious Broadcasters evangelicals gained a share of sustaining time and freedom to purchase radio time. The impending monopoly of the Federal Council was broken. Evangelicals were assured a voice on the air.

The task of educating radio and television leaders concerning the differences between the Federal Council of Churches (or its successor, the National Council of Churches) and the National Association of Evangelicals was no easy assignment. The NRB helped immeasurably. But all of the problems are not yet solved. In 1956 the Broadcasting and Film Commission of the National Council of Churches passed a resolution calling upon the radio and television industries to allocate free time for non-partisan religious broadcasts. This was the way, the Commission said, to eliminate "irresponsible racketeering religious broadcasts." The industries have apparently ignored the recommendation but apprehension and tension continue.

Other problems which face today's gospel broadcaster are the cancellation of network and local religious programs, the relegation of religious programs to less desirable times, the industry's preoccupation with ratings, and the gradual disappearance of network option time. Since the advances in the television industry, many radio stations have specialized in music, news, or other non-religious features. It is difficult to get religious programs on a station concerned with an image.

In spite of problems, however, thanks to NRB, evangelical broadcasts such as The Lutheran Hour, The Hour of Decision, Back to the Bible Hour, and The Old Fashioned Revival Hour continue to proclaim the Word of Truth. To help meet the challenge of our times the twentieth annual convention of the

National Religious Broadcasters in January 1963 organized the International Christian Broadcasters. The new body is occupied with relations between the World Conference on Missionary Communications and the NRB. It is further evidence of evangelical commitment to the task of proclaiming the gospel to our world.

Christian Nurture

A second major interest of the NAE and its affiliated organizations is the educational task of the churches. The New Testament makes clear that evangelism must be followed by edification. Evangelicals therefore directed their new-found strength to lifting the sagging Sunday school movement.

The history of the American Sunday school movement between the two great wars is no striking success story. In 1916 American churches reported 20,000,000 pupils attending Sunday school. By 1945 this figure had grown to 24,000,000 but when compared to population growth the percentage of America's children in Sunday school had dropped from 19.6 per cent in 1916 to 17.6 per cent in 1945.

Many conservative Christians were unhappy with the liberal stress on the goodness of unregenerated men and the rejection of the unique inspiration of the Bible found in much of the literature produced by the International Council of Religious Education. Gone, too, were the giant Sunday school rallies of an earlier day which fired Christian workers with enthusiasm for the teaching of the Bible.

When the NAE was born evangelicals were especially mindful of the curriculum trends within the International Council of Religious Education. The Council's uniform lessons presented liberal theology and the social gospel with little if any reference to the Bible. Because of this trend, the National Association of Evangelicals in 1943 appointed Dr. Clarence H. Benson to head a new committee to develop an evangelical system of uniform Sunday school lessons.

A number of evangelicals concerned about the doctrinal drift within the International Council of Religious Education met with the Church School Commission of the NAE in Columbus, Ohio, in April 1944. These Christian education leaders proposed that a new Sunday school association be organized which would adhere strictly to evangelical principles. The outgrowth of this meeting was the formation of the National Sunday School Association the following year.

The first national convention of the NSSA was held in Chicago's Moody Church, October 2-6, 1946. Audiences ranged from 400 to a high of 4,000 on Saturday night. Attendance at the convention assured NSSA leaders that many churches were aware of the potential of the Sunday school and were concerned about what could be done for their congregations through the Sunday schools.

At its inception the National Sunday School Association was related to the National Association of Evangelicals through its Church School Commission, which was composed of the members of the executive committee of the NSSA. To assure its doctrinal integrity the new organization also adopted the NAE statement of belief.

The first and foremost objective of the NSSA was the production of the new uniform lesson plans. A lesson committee of ten was chosen to work on the project. Members of this committee represented Presbyterian, Baptist, Disciples of Christ, Free Methodist, Plymouth Brethren, Assemblies of God, and Lutheran denominations. An Advisory Committee of One Hundred, consisting of educational leaders, pastors, Sunday school teachers and leaders, editors, publishers and lesson writers from major denominations, was chosen to work with the lesson committee.

The committee adopted a policy as a guide for its work which included the winning of pupils to Jesus Christ and the submission of their lives to the will of God as major objectives

and the capacities and ages of pupils as significant considerations in the selection of Bible-centered lessons.

Sunday, January 4, 1948, marked a new day in Sunday
school literature as a million pupils began using the new NSSA
uniform lessons. Today an estimated 3,000,000 pupils are using
the uniform lessons provided by ten publishers. In recent
years, however, NSSA has given equal support to the graded
materials of leading publishing houses.

While the need for Sunday school materials was a major
factor in bringing into existence the National Sunday School
Association, it was soon evident that there was much to be done
which did not directly involve curriculum. Sunday school
leaders discovered that if the movement was to advance, it
needed local leadership. They, therefore, tried to spark local
enthusiasm. During the following years promotional slogans
read: "Revitalize the American Sunday School" and "Revival
Now Through the Sunday School."

The major advances in the National Sunday School Association, however, have occurred through the national conventions
held in strategic locations throughout the country. These conventions have been high points for pastors, Sunday school
teachers and Christian education leaders from across the nation.
In 1945 few Sunday school conventions were held anywhere.
Since that time NSSA has had occasion to report a new Sunday
school association formed directly or indirectly by the Association in some part of the nation every four months. As a consequence many metropolitan areas have initiated conventions just
for the churches in their own locality.

Sunday school conventions have been a means of sharing the
vision of how a vibrant Sunday school can transform a church.
Each convention is composed of two types of meetings: (1)
Inspirational meetings provide the zeal to undertake the task of
building a strong Sunday school. (2) Workshops advance the
proper methods for doing the job in the best possible way.

Increased enthusiasm and growth mark the recent national

conventions. In 1955 twin conventions were held, one on the east coast and one on the west coast. The 1961 convention, meeting in Detroit, had a registration of 10,000 with an attendance of over 20,000. Sparked by this new zeal NSSA, by 1960, maintained 21 affiliated city Sunday school associations, 17 area associations, and 8 state associations. In that year its budget topped $100,000.

In addition to the giant conventions NSSA sponsors several special weeks during the year to emphasize youth, the family, and the Sunday school. These programs help the church to reach the family and the community for Christ. The attendance crusade "March to Sunday School in March" has proved to be one of the most popular projects of NSSA. The Association's *Link,* a monthly magazine, also provides helpful information for the Sunday school leader.

In recent years several commissions of the NSSA have reflected the vigor of the Association and have helped to revitalize many churches and Sunday schools in America. Among these are the Research Commission, the Camp Commission, the Youth Commission, the Denominational Sunday School Secretaries, the Area Chairmen Commission and the affiliated body, The National Directors of Christian Education. In recent years these commissions meeting prior to the national conventions have added to NSSA depth, vision, and creativity.

Today, after two decades, thanks to NSSA, the Bible is once again the textbook of many Sunday schools. Though liberal theology's influence had all but taken the Bible out of many Sunday schools, evangelical leaders united in believing that the Sunday school was the proper place to teach the Bible as the revealed Word of God. Moreover, the Sunday school in many evangelical churches has once again become an evangelistic agency. Enrollment and attendance are steadily increasing as a result of promotion of Sunday school and improved Bible teaching. In 1960 American churches reported 39,500,000 pupils or 22 per cent of the population in Sunday school. NSSA may not be the major factor in this increase but it is certainly an important one.

Another NAE affiliate vitally engaged in Christian education is the National Association of Christian Schools. By the end of World War II a growing number of Christian parents were finding fault with the public school system. They disliked the evidence of a progressive philosophy of education; they felt the public schools were failing to provide adequate moral values; and they interpreted a series of U. S. Supreme Court decisions (especially the McCollum Case in 1948) as endorsements of secularism and humanism.

At first these parents tried to enroll their children in Christian schools operated by Lutheran or Reformed churches. This influx, however, moved the National Union of Christian Schools, a Reformed association, to request the NAE in 1947 to consider the establishment of an organization to meet the needs of these conservative Christians. Moving quickly, the NAE organized on May 13, 1947, the National Association of Christian Schools to promote the establishment of new Christian day schools throughout the country.

During the early formative years of the NACS, Dr. Mark Fakkema, who had given leadership to the Reformed school system, served as educational director. Under Fakkema's guidance the Association by 1955 counted 123 affiliated schools with 12,187 pupils. The NACS continues today under Mr. John Blanchard's leadership as an affiliated organization of NAE and as a channel of evangelical educational interests.

A third center of evangelical action in education is the Education Commission of NAE. Acting in an advisory and executive capacity, the Commission seeks to strengthen and increase the educational resources available to evangelicals. It acts as a clearing house for information concerning opportunities for study and reviews the qualifications of schools seeking membership in the NAE. In its evaluation it takes stock of the school's physical plant, its future growth plans, its equipment, its training, and the sufficiency of its faculty.

NAE began to assume an interest in higher education in 1943. When the Commission on Education was created Dr. Stephen W. Paine, President of Houghton College in New York, provided significant leadership in the new endeavor. The Commission originally functioned in four areas: (1) liberal arts colleges, (2) theological seminaries, (3) Bible institutes and Bible colleges, and (4) secondary schools.

In the years that followed probably NAE's most significant contribution to the cause of Christian education was the report of its Commission on a Christian Philosophy of Education created in 1946. The final report of this committee was delivered to the NAE convention in 1951. Under the direction of Dr. Frank Gaebelein, headmaster of the Stony Brook School, the volume *Christian Education in a Democracy* was published by Oxford Press and presented to the evangelical public. The volume provided a blueprint for evangelical education for more than a decade.

The seminary section of the Education Commission works for increased cooperation among its member schools and toward strengthened lines of liaison with the American Association of Theological Schools, the only accrediting agency for theological schools. From time to time talk of the need for a conservative seminary accrediting agency arises, but as long as the AATS does not base accreditation on any particular theological viewpoint there seems to be little reason for another agency.

In 1944, however, the Commission did give birth to the North American Association of Bible Institutes and Bible Colleges. The purposes of this Association were to bring into cooperative fellowship all Bible institutes and Bible colleges with similar objectives, to establish general standards to facilitate interchange of credits, and to maintain records of administrators and teachers. During the years of its existence the NAABIBC made clear the unique educational philosophy of the Bible institutes and colleges and sparked a new educational enthusiasm in the member schools. In 1947, however, the Accrediting Association of Bible Institutes and Bible Colleges was organized at Winona Lake, Indiana, for the specific purpose of accreditation. Most of the schools in the NAABIBC were soon active in this more comprehensive body and as a result the NAABIBC was discontinued.

In 1957 the Education Commission took another significant step. It formed a committee for a new translation of the Bible. That committee is still actively pursuing its goal.

These are only some of the contributions of the Education Commission of the NAE. The Commission continues to grapple with today's needs and to make evangelical education a significant part of today's Christian endeavor.

Missions

A third area of evangelical concern which found expression in NAE is the foreign missionary enterprise. Prior to 1942 the Foreign Missions Conference of North America had served a wide spectrum of missionary agencies. In the early 1940's, however, unrest was evident. Liberal influence in numerous denominational boards and societies had a disquieting effect. The number of new missionaries sent to the field, FMC reports showed, was declining. Furthermore, a high percentage were going for technical specialization rather than evangelism and church planting.

Then the merger idea appeared. Enthusiasts for missionary ecumenicity regarded the older voluntary society idea employed in the FMC as *passé*. They called for a more closely knit organization and more church control. Though temporarily stymied in their plans at Buck Hill Falls in 1949, the advocates of organized ecumenicity devised plans for creating a Division of Foreign Missions within the newly projected National Council of Churches which would begin to operate in spite of the continued resistance of FMC. At this point the sizeable Southern Baptist

Foreign Mission Board voted to withdraw from the FMC "and thus leave the conference to make such changes in its structure and functions as a majority of its members may deem suitable to their needs." At about the same time a number of other conservative mission groups also withdrew from the FMC.

When the National Association of Evangelicals was organized in 1943, a group of conservative mission agencies and "faith" boards naturally gravitated toward one another in order to accomplish common goals. Consequently the NAE created a Department of Home and Foreign Missions to serve those groups outside of the FMC. To assist in this missionary endeavor the NAE opened an Office of Affairs in Washington, D.C., headed by Dr. Clyde W. Taylor, a former missionary to Latin America under the Christian and Missionary Alliance. The scope of the missionary task, however, soon demanded a broader base of cooperation.

Mission leaders within NAE issued a call to 75 mission groups asking them to send representatives to a conference in Chicago in May 1945. At this meeting, held in the Stevens Hotel, a committee was appointed to draw up a constitution and a set of bylaws. This action was then reported to the NAE convention also meeting at that time in the city.

The Evangelical Foreign Missions Association adopted its Constitution on September 19, 1945, and legal incorporation followed in Delaware on December 29, 1945. By April 1946, the EFMA assembled for its first annual convention in Minneapolis, Minnesota. There 15 boards were received as members of the Association. EFMA has proved so successful in its ministry that by June 1966 it was serving over 100 mission boards (63 of which were members) and 14,000 missionaries (6,452 of these being from the 63 member boards).

EFMA was established to provide a triple service to its constituents: (1) to make adequate provision for the procurement of all types of missionary documents and to provide diplomatic information needed by mission boards, (2) to operate a New York City purchasing office which serves homeland Christian workers as well as missionaries, and (3) to provide for the travel needs of missionaries and mission executives. Today the Washington office of the EFMA also receives and channels funds for those overseas evangelical agencies which have no office in the U.S.A.

In addition to these duties it provides official representation of its member missions before foreign governments, a few remaining colonial offices, and the many departments of the United States government. This service might be the obtaining of a visa for a missionary in India, assisting endangered missionaries in Ecuador, or appealing for religious freedom in Spain. Religious liberty of minority groups in foreign lands often demands EFMA's support. In these endeavors the Association has the privilege of leaning on NAE when such a constituency is needed as a basis of authority in seeking government service here or abroad.

What has this evangelical cooperation accomplished? (1) In missionary expenditures for equipment and supplies, EFMA has saved her member societies thousands of dollars. For instance, in the five-year period from 1952-1957, EFMA saved foreign missionary workers and organizations over $125,000. In November 1965, the EFMA Purchasing Office reported reaching in a recent twelve-month period over $1,000,000 in purchases for Christian workers, churches, and evangelical organizations.

(2) EFMA also sponsors conferences covering the various fields of missionary endeavor. Among these, the annual retreat for mission executives is especially significant. These gatherings have become the strategy sessions for planning the evangelical world missionary thrust.

Along this line EFMA was responsible for the conference in 1951 which established Evangelical Literature Overseas, the agency which unites evangelical missionary literature efforts.

Four years later (1955) the Executive Secretary of EFMA attended a literature conference called by ELO in Costa Rica. Characterized by a oneness of mind the conference delegates joined in the formation of LEAL (*Literatura Evangelica para America Latina*), a cooperative venture in the production and distribution of evangelical literature for Spanish-speaking countries. EFMA encouraged all evangelical missions to cooperate.

(3) In 1954 EFMA established the *Missionary News Service*. Published semi-monthly and covering the mission fields of the world from an evangelical viewpoint, its purpose is to provide mission board executives, editors, and other evangelical leaders in our country with up-to-date missionary statistics and news stories.

To gain its missionary statistics EFMA conducts surveys on various evangelical levels of cooperation and joins with other national and international bodies. Through its committee, it was in charge of making the first complete survey of evangelical Spanish literature and editing the first literature catalogue in that language. By 1958 the organization had completed two such Spanish literature surveys. These were followed in 1961 by *Protestant Missions in Latin America—A Statistical Survey* edited by Clyde W. Taylor and Wade T. Coggins.

(4) Among the recent outstanding accomplishments of EFMA none holds more significance for the future than the cooperative ventures it has undertaken with the Interdenominational Foreign Missions Association, a fundamental mission association founded in 1917 and composed of 44 non-denominational boards.

By 1957, when the two organizations were contributing 56 per cent of all the Protestant missionaries in Latin America, both felt the need for greater cooperation and unity. As a consequence the two bodies called a conference in December 1957, which was attended by 37 executives representing 24 missions. At this conference the participants voted to establish the Evangelical Committee for Latin America (ECLA) for the purpose of encouraging action at the national level, by missions and national churches, to speed the evangelization of this great area. From this experience in cooperation the two groups realized that they could helpfully work together without organic union.

A similar venture was undertaken in Nairobi, Kenya, in 1963 when the new African Evangelical Office was opened through the joint sponsorship of EFMA and IFMA. Its purpose is to encourage Christian unity through evangelical cooperation. Mr. Kenneth Downing of the Africa Inland Mission is general secretary of the group.

This was followed by three other significant joint projects: the Church Growth Seminars directed by Dr. Donald McGavran, the *Evangelical Missions Quarterly* under the editorship of James Reapsome, editor of *The Sunday Times,* and the creation of CAMEO, the Committee to Assist Missionary Education Overseas. By December 1964, there were five joint committees of EFMA and IFMA. But their greatest achievement was then only in the planning stages, a Congress on the Church's Worldwide Mission.

After the merger of the International Missionary Conference with the World Council of Churches at New Delhi in 1961, evangelical mission leaders felt that they needed increased cooperation and a major convention to establish working guidelines for future missionary labor. As a result 938 delegates—missionaries, national churchmen, mission executives, professors of missions, students, and pastors—from 71 different countries and 150 mission boards attended the Congress at Wheaton, Illinois, in April 1966. They met to reaffirm the scriptural basis for the church's commission, to come to terms with the issues of an ecumenical age, to hear of the Spirit's working among the earth's three billion inhabitants, and to declare their position on such challenging issues as the new face of Roman Catholicism and the evangelical's social responsibility.

From the Congress emerged a document called the Wheaton Declaration. Summarizing the work of 25 discussion groups and the delivery of 15 major study papers, the Declaration deals with: syncretism, the new universalism, proselytization, Roman Catholicism, church growth, foreign missions, evangelical unity, evaluating methods of missionary work, social concern, and the church in a hostile world.

A significant paragraph from the statement on unity asserts: "We shall encourage evangelical mission mergers when such will eliminate duplication of administration, produce more efficient stewardship of personnel and resources and strengthen their ministries . . . we caution evangelicals to avoid establishing new churches or organizations where existing groups of like precious faith satisfactorily fill the role."

The Congress shows that evangelical missions are united in the foundations of their faith and in their responsibility to carry the gospel of liberating grace to the masses of earth. Just how great a difference the Congress will make on the mission fields remains to be seen. Much depends on the various missions as they seek to implement the work of the Congress. This much is clear: EFMA and IFMA have pointed toward a new day of unity among conservative evangelicals.

Social Concern

One of the most significant developments within American conservatism since World War II is its awakened interest in humanitarian causes. Fundamentalism's reaction to liberalism's social gospel left American evangelicalism off balance in its stand on Biblical social responsibility. Any form of welfare or humanitarianism was too often quickly dismissed as "utopian" or, worst of all, a veiled expression of the "social gospel." Social disintegration was in some circles made an article in conservatism's creed. Human suffering was a sign of the times, an inescapable prelude to the second coming of Christ.

World War II, however, seemed to arouse evangelicalism from its social stupor. Many evangelical leaders agreed with Carl F. H. Henry who wrote in 1947 of *The Uneasy Conscience of Modern Fundamentalism*. Henry called for the application of the gospel in the sphere of social welfare. Can modern man, he asked, drifting in a sea of relativism find any adequate ethical life apart from the guiding light of Biblical revelation?

Since the formation of NAE, evangelicals have sought to stress the relevancy of the gospel in humanitarian efforts without using the churches as tools of social or political reform. The primary task of the churches is the preaching of the gospel. But when the Association's Committee on Policy and Fields Endeavor reported to the Constitutional Convention in 1943 it assumed that evangelicals could not ignore moral questions. It therefore called for a program of "war services."

At the 1944 convention in Columbus, Ohio, a Committee for Postwar Relief began to accept donations of food and clothing. Before the war had ended the warehouse of the Committee was filled with gifts for homeless and starving Europeans. When these and subsequent gifts were distributed a tract or gospel message accompanied it. Usually evangelical churches in the war-torn countries assumed responsibility for the distribution of the food and clothing. In these ways evangelicals tried to assure that the "cup of cold water" was offered in Jesus' name.

The Committee for Postwar Relief was officially recognized and chartered at the NAE convention in 1945. Relief work continued in Europe until 1950 when the Korean conflict broadened NAE's relief ministry and necessitated a change in the Commission's name. The World Relief Commission (WRC) thus became an integral part of the NAE and not merely an approved organization.

One of the first functions of the WRC was to initiate a working arrangement with the large Central Mennonite Relief

Agency. Material relief totaling millions of dollars began pouring into war-racked Korea. It seemed, however, that no matter how much was given, so much more was needed. The total giving of all Americans failed to supply the barest essentials for the stricken South Koreans.

Nevertheless, the Commission continued to receive gifts for overseas distribution and thereby to express in some measure evangelical compassion. The need for and the unique importance of the WRC were well expressed in an editorial appearing in *United Evangelical Action* (1957): "The World Relief Commission, as the instrument of the National Association of Evangelicals, distributes hundreds of thousands of dollars worth of clothing and food every year but this relief—and that of all other relief agencies in the world—is but a fraction of the help needed by suffering people. . . . NAE relief is different—it is Christian relief. With every gift of food and clothing distributed overseas by reliable, established evangelical Christians, goes a gospel message in printed form."

The 1950's also saw the social concern of evangelicals give birth to several welfare agencies across our own country. One work began in Chicago when a local group tried to place children in worthy homes but were hindered by the State of Illinois until it was sponsored by a national organization. Following its appeal to the NAE and its consequent sponsorship, the new group was recognized and licensed. Scores of unwanted children were soon placed in Christian homes.

At the NAE convention in 1951 it was apparent that another commission was needed to coordinate the work of such welfare agencies. Thus, the Commission on Social Action was created. Shortly thereafter welfare agencies appeared in Los Angeles and in New York. The southern California work, a child of the NAE regional office, has since 1956 placed over 500 babies in Christian homes. The most recent welfare organization related to NAE is Evangelical Family Service in Syracuse, New York.

The Social Action Commission also embraces as its concern the older gospel missions ministry. By 1958, 250 missions were members of the International Union of Gospel Missions. Ruben Lores, a Latin-American missionary, voiced the reasons for this Christian concern for humanity when he wrote: "Certainly the primary function of the church is a spiritual ministry to the world. And yet I believe the social responsibility is included in that spiritual responsibility. The Church as an organization is an important part of organized society that cannot and should not desire to remain neutral to social responsibility. Neutrality on the part of the Church would be construed as the negation of the redemptive truth we proclaim." An increasing number of conservative-minded Christians were agreeing.

By 1955 the World Relief Commission's ministry had so expanded that a full-time director and staff were appointed. Mr. Wendell L. Rockey became the new director of the Commission and two new relief processing centers opened in Modesto, California, and Nappanee, Indiana. The WRC soon joined hands with Northwest Korean Relief for continued aid to South Korea; and Haiti and Taiwan called for evangelical assistance. By November 15, 1956, *United Evangelical Action* reported that "Christian relief through the World Relief Commission had gone to Austria, Belgium, China, Czechoslovakia, England, Finland, France, Formosa, Germany, Greece, Holland, Indo-China, Italy, Japan, Korea, Norway, the Philippines, Poland, Rumania, and Trans-Jordan." This was quite an accomplishment for a twelve-year-old organization.

In 1956 the WRC qualified for U.S. government surplus foods. Membership in the International Cooperation Administration and access to government surplus food came just in time for the WRC to provide assistance for the Hungarian refugees from the short-lived rebellion against Communist control in 1956.

Compared to older and larger Christian relief ministries the work of the WRC is not impressive. For example, in 1960

Roman Catholic relief reached $60,000,000 and that of the World Council of Churches $14,000,000 while WRC relief totaled only $353,158. To the WRC figure, however, must be added the work of other evangelical endeavors. Under the direction of Bob Pierce, a former war correspondent in Korea, World Vision, a member of EFMA, combines evangelism and social welfare in its program centered in Asia; and Compassion Incorporated, which arose out of the Everett Swanson Evangelistic Association, has assumed a sizeable Korean orphan work. If these and other such groups were included in a single evangelical figure, the sum would be much greater. Yet by 1964 the figure for WRC gifts alone topped the half million mark.

The current conflict in Viet Nam offers a new challenge to the ministry of NAE's Relief Commission. The WRC has established in that strife-torn country a Christian Lay Leadership Training Center. The basic objectives of this school are four: (1) on-the-job agricultural training, (2) assistance for orphans and youth, (3) teaching of Christianity, and (4) development of self-help. The Center is providing basic facilities for young Vietnamese to learn trades and crafts by which they can help their fellow countrymen to help themselves. From its headquarters in the central highlands of Viet Nam it also distributes food to many starving tribesmen. With the cooperation of the South Vietnamese government a minimum of 1,500,000 pounds of food will be distributed in the economically deficient areas of central Viet Nam during 1966-67.

While the evangelical ministry of world relief and social concern is not all that NAE leaders envision, it is nevertheless a significant service to the suffering masses of our shattered world. As long as the World Relief Commission continues the distribution of millions of pounds of food and clothing and the Commission on Social Action stimulates welfare services at home, NAE will provide a convincing refutation of the charge, "Evangelicals do not care."

Space does not allow further elaboration of other NAE ministries, such as the Commission on Chaplains, which is the endorsing agency for nearly a score of denominations, or the annual seminars in Washington, D.C., on the role of government. Surely, however, the major concerns of the NAE are clear to all. Surely we can see how the past twenty-five years have vindicated the vision of the founders of the Association and have brought to it a significant measure of maturity.

6: American
Evangelicalism Today

"Something has been happening within Fundamentalism," Arnold W. Hearn announced in a 1958 issue of the *Christian Century*. "Away from the centers of ecclesiastical power and theological education in the major denominations, there has been a remarkable renascence of intellectual activity among fundamentalist scholars."

Something has indeed been happening within post-World War II "fundamentalism." On every hand the observer of American evangelicalism can find evidence of ferment. A certain restlessness characterizes the movement today. Much of this is due to dissatisfaction with the drift of fundamentalism between the two great wars. The vast majority of today's critics within evangelicalism have no serious objections to the original doctrines of fundamentalism but they feel that after World War I the movement veered sharply from its original course and stumbled into the mire of some unfortunate emphases.

"The New Evangelicalism"

As early as 1947, when the new voice in conservatism was a mere whisper, Carl F. H. Henry in his book *The Uneasy Conscience of Modern Fundamentalism* made it clear that in chiding fundamentalism's lack of social concern he was not taking a slap at fundamental doctrines. Henry wrote in the

111

preface to this book, "Those who read with competence will know that the 'uneasy conscience' of which I write is not one troubled about the great biblical verities, which I consider the only outlook capable of resolving our problems, but rather one distressed by the frequent failure to apply them effectively to crucial problems confronting the modern mind. It is an application of, not a revolt against, fundamentals of the faith, for which I plead."

Henry apparently had his finger on the pulse of conservatism because the restless fever continued. A. W. Tozer, editor of the *Alliance Witness* and a highly respected voice in conservative circles, said in 1954, "In my opinion fundamentalism has been retrogressing rapidly during the last 20 years." Tozer went on to compare fundamentalists with army worms. "Fundamentalist leaders, like these army worms, have for decades been following each other around the rim of their own little jars, each one afraid to step aside or hunt any new direction for himself, each slavishly following the other."

Criticism of fundamentalism was not in itself anything new. Leaders within the traditional denominations, some of them evangelical, had for decades been pointing out fundamentalism's schismatic spirit. This was to be expected from those charged with the advancement of denominational unity. The new critics, however, spoke from an attachment to the basic beliefs of fundamentalism and from within its interdenominational perspective.

Moreover, the voices decrying the excesses or imbalances of fundamentalism swelled to a chorus in the 1950's. The movement's "wowser" worship, its cultural isolationism, its sectarian separatism, its monastic ethics, its theological hair-splitting— these and other characteristics were relentlessly exposed.

In back of most of these criticisms, we must stress, was a desire to lift the fundamental faith of evangelicalism out of the shoals of strife and negation on which it nearly foundered in the 1920's and to redirect it toward positive contemporary objectives. The critics—most of them really engaging in self-criticism —suggested that like the young man in the gospel story, it could be said of fundamentalism, "Yet one thing thou lackest." Fundamentalism sought to safeguard God's message from the waves of modernistic unbelief. But it neglected the need of propelling that message into the social and intellectual life of the world. Many evangelicals are now giving themselves to this task but they want it understood that in no way should their work be construed as a departure from the "fundamentals" of the faith.

The objectives of this new wing of American evangelicalism were fairly clearly defined in 1960 by Harold John Ockenga. In an article entitled "Resurgent Evangelical Leadership" in *Christianity Today*, he wrote, "The evangelical has general objectives he wishes to see achieved. One of them is a revival of Christianity in the midst of a secular world. . . . The evangelical wishes to retrieve Christianity from a mere eddy of the main stream into the full current of modern life. He desires to win a new respectability for orthodoxy in the academic circles by producing scholars who can defend the faith on intellectual ground. He hopes to recapture denominational leadership from within the denominations rather than abandoning those denominations to modernism. He intends to restate his position carefully and cogently so that it must be considered in the theological dialogue. He intends that Christianity will be the mainspring in many of the reforms of the societal order. It is wrong to abdicate responsibility for society under the impetus of a theology which overemphasizes the eschatological."

Taking our cue, then, from Dr. Ockenga we can summarize the basic objectives of the new evangelicalism as a quest of (1) academic respectability, (2) social involvement, and (3) denominational redirection.

To what degree has a revitalized evangelicalism achieved these goals? What evidence is there for a new vitality in conservative circles? Several lines of evidence suggest a significant degree of achievement.

First, this revitalized evangelicalism has infused a new vigor into conservative scholarship. Fundamentalism of the 1920's and 1930's, with a few notable exceptions, was not able to match the intellectual level of the earlier leaders of the movement.

Norman F. Furniss, in his *Fundamentalist Controversy 1918-1931,* is undoubtedly biased in some of his remarks but he strikes uncomfortably close to the truth when he writes, "Except for J. Gresham Machen and a few others, the conservatives had no leader with an impressive training. Its champions were men whose principal assets were conviction and zeal, not erudition, . . . Ignorance, then, was a feature of the movement; it became a badge the orthodox wore proudly. They believed that faith was God's only demand upon His people and that higher education was of limited value, even a handicap in seeking the Kingdom."

The new evangelical, too, feels that fundamentalism between the wars was too often occupied with that well-established sport among Americans, the sniping at intellectuals. As a result it failed to keep pace with the changes in modern society and insulated itself against the broader currents of American life. These contemporary conservatives are determined to change all of this. And to a significant degree they are succeeding.

In his article in the *Christian Century* Arnold W. Hearn makes this reluctant admission: "A new generation of earnest intellectuals is appearing within the ranks of avowedly fundamentalist groups and educational institutions. . . . They are able to view other kinds of theology more objectively and appreciatively than their predecessors did in the 1920's, and to deal responsibly with these theologies from the standpoint of their own presuppositions."

This new academic excitement can be seen in the level of instruction in fundamental schools and in their quest for accreditation whether as Bible colleges, Christian liberal arts colleges, or theological seminaries. It can also be observed in the clear articulation of the evangelical view of Scripture as the Word of God written. In the volume *Revelation and the Bible* a number of evangelical essayists defend the Bible in its original manuscripts as the absolute, normative, inerrant and verbalized revelation of God. While written in the style of prose and poetry, in allegorical, literal and typological speech, in the language and idiom of divinely selected men, the Scriptures are nevertheless the infallible disclosure of God's mind, will, and plan for men.

The spark for much of this Biblical study in conservative quarters has come from The Evangelical Theological Society which now numbers 800 members and is responsible for encouraging conservative scholarship in Biblical and theological areas.

The breadth of this conservative renewal is revealed in the volume *Contemporary Evangelical Thought.* Published in 1957, the book presents essays from leading evangelical scholars dealing with Christian ethics, Christian education, Biblical revelation, philosophy and religion, evangelism, ecumenicity, preaching, science, and philosophies of history.

Many of the new evangelicals feel that fundamentalism proved especially vulnerable in its battle with evolutionism. In the hopes of lifting the evangelical reputation touching science, a number of conservatives have spoken to the issue of a philosophy of science. In 1954 Bernard Ramm's *The Christian View of Science and Scripture* pioneered in this area. Ramm adopted a view he called "progressive creationism which teaches that over the millions of years of geological history God has been fiatly creating higher and higher forms of life." In addition to Ramm, Edward John Carnell, John W. Klotz, Carl F. H. Henry, Gordon H. Clark, and Russell L. Mixter have contributed to this discussion concerned with Christianity and science.

To mark the centennial of Charles Darwin's *The Origin of Species*, Dr. Mixter of Wheaton College edited a volume called

Evolution and Christian Thought Today. Contributors included scientists from leading universities across the United States such as Walter R. Hearn, professor of chemistry at Iowa State University, Wilbur L. Bullock, professor of zoology at the University of New Hampshire, and V. Elving Anderson from the Dight Institute for Human Genetics at the University of Minnesota. These men along with 800 others make up the American Scientific Affiliation, a group of evangelical Christians professionally trained and active in scientific work.

This resurgence of conservatism in America has also reactivated evangelical publishing. The list of magazines reflecting this vitality would include *His, Eternity, United Evangelical Action, Decision, Christian Life,* and a score of others. New strength in scholarship can also be found in orthodox journals such as *Christianity Today, The Reformed Journal, Bibliotheca Sacra, Bulletin of the Evangelical Theological Society, Journal of the American Scientific Affiliation* and the *Gordon Review.* The number of solid Biblical studies, biographies, and devotional books written by evangelicals and published by a variety of publishers during the last ten years can now be numbered in the hundreds.

When all of this evidence—and more—is accumulated any unprejudiced observer of American evangelicalism is forced to conclude that the movement is marked by a new intellectual vigor.

Less prominent but nevertheless noteworthy is the continuing effort to prod the social conscience of evangelicalism. As we have already observed (Chapter 5), in the 1920's and 30's many fundamentalists considered social decline a mark of the last days, an inescapable prelude to the second coming of Christ. Conservatives often shunned social involvement as the poison of the "social gospelers."

Such views are by no means dead but the new evangelical leaders regard this attitude as tantamount to encouraging social injustice and deterioration. While in no sense embracing the liberal theology that assigns evil in the world to certain social institutions, they plead for the application of the gospel in the more constructive spheres of social welfare. Carl F. H. Henry remains one of the leading spokesmen in this area, contending that the Biblical verities are the only sure bases for the ethical life and social action. Henry develops his ideas further in his *Aspects of Christian Social Ethics* and *The God Who Shows Himself*.

In recent months Professor Lewis B. Smedes of Calvin College has engaged Dr. Henry in a friendly yet vigorous discussion through the pages of *The Reformed Journal* and *Eternity* magazine. From his evangelical perspective in the Reformed tradition Dr. Smedes insists that Dr. Henry does not have a social ethic. He has a personal ethic for regenerate individuals but no ethic that prescribes a way of action for human society. Smedes feels that evangelicals must move beyond humanitarianism and philanthropy to an ethic which prescribes a manner of life for society.

This type of informed discussion, conducted in an irenic spirit, can only strengthen the evangelical witness and stimulate other volumes like David O. Moberg's *Inasmuch: Christian Social Responsibility in the Twentieth Century* and Foy Valentine's *The Cross in the Marketplace*.

The work of the National Association of Evangelicals from its beginnings, as we have seen, accented the relevancy of the gospel in humanitarian efforts. It has sponsored industrial chaplains; it has engaged in war relief in Europe, Korea, and currently in Viet Nam; and three years before the U. S. Supreme Court made its historic decision touching school desegregation NAE's Social Action Commission declared that segregation is not lawfully Christian and "evangelicals are obliged to press the case against segregation simultaneously with evangelism." Critics may find fault with the bases and extent of evangelical social involvement; they cannot contest the new interest in social issues.

Finally, the new evangelical leaders reflect current concern for Christian unity in their criticisms of separatism. After the modernist-fundamentalist conflict in the 1920's two basic views of Christian cooperation emerged in conservative circles. The American Council of Christian Churches founded in 1941 under the Rev. Carl McIntire's leadership was "militantly pro-Gospel and anti-Modernist." Its constitution barred individual churches and denominations from its membership as long as any of them were associated with the Federal Council of Churches or its successor, the National Council of Churches. The ACCC was thus an exclusivist or separatist organization.

The National Association of Evangelicals from its birth tried to follow a different course to unity. Its members were not required to separate from denominations or churches affiliated with the Federal Council. Moreover, leaders of the NAE endeavored to refrain from the American Council's militant attack upon the Federal Council and the National Council. Operating under its principles the ACCC has rallied only 200,000 members since 1941; NAE has grown to 2,500,000.

Neither of these organizations, however, has gained the unqualified support of certain leaders of the new evangelicalism. Many of the new breed oppose fundamentalism's fragmentizing tendencies. They deplore that spirit of independency which lauds separation from other Christian groups as a badge of courage and conviction. They have not evidenced wholehearted support for NAE because they find even it excessively exclusive.

On the other hand, these architects of the new way do not give their approval to the National Council of Churches or to the World Council of Churches. The best they have been able to advance concerning Christian unity thus far is the fundamentalist strategy of the 1920's. They believe evangelicals should seek to recapture denominational leadership by a program of infiltration. In his article "Resurgent Evangelical Leadership" Dr. Ockenga urges, "It is time for firm evangelicals to seize their opportunity to minister in and influence the modernist groups. Why is it incredible that the evangelicals should be able to infiltrate the denominations and strengthen the things that remain, and possibly resume control of such denominations?"

Unlike many fundamentalists, the new evangelicals see clearly the dangers in unhindered independency as well as the dangers in church unionism. The best discussion of this whole problem of Biblical unity comes from Carl F. H. Henry's pen. In four articles for *Christianity Today* in 1956, Henry discussed the perils of independency and the perils of ecumenicity. He revealed how each of these movements has its own tensions. "Independency tends to be intolerant, Church Unionism to be tolerant. The former moves in the direction of exclusivism, the latter toward inclusivism. One holds a low view of the Church in its visible and historical aspects, and the other a high view. The one glorifies separateness, while the other reaches out toward ecclesiasticism. Independency remains highly creedal in minute detail, while Church Unionism becomes vague and ill-defined in theological basis. One can easily become Pharisaic, the other Sadducean." Henry himself apparently favors a "transdenominational" approach to unity and has been providing such a voice in *Christianity Today*.

As is true in almost any human endeavor these new ideas within the ranks of American conservatism have not been advanced without resistance. Criticisms of fundamentalism's wealth of pugilistic tactics and poverty of respectable scholarship aroused the ire of certain staunch fundamentalists. Heated retorts were launched against the leaders of the new way in evangelicalism, calling them mind-worshippers and subversives seeking to surrender fundamentalism to modernism. These critical fundamentalists loaded the term "neo-evangelical" (originally coined by Harold John Ockenga to distinguish the new movement from fundamentalism, liberalism, and neo-orthodoxy) with an assortment of nasty implications and then pinned it on various evangelical leaders and institutions.

By 1960 two camps without definite boundaries were vaguely discernible. The first group, who wore the title "fundamentalist" proudly, insisted that the second group was making a subtle retreat to liberalism. The second group, usually called "new evangelicals," claimed that the first group was by its attitude and temperament severing itself from true historic evangelicalism.

The ferment engendered by the dissatisfaction with certain aspects of fundamentalism continues to bubble within interdenominational evangelicalism. Many orthodox Christians refuse to be caught up in the swirl. Labels, they know, are convenient for purposes of identification and simplification but are never adequate for communicating an individual's beliefs. It is safe to say that many conservative Christians find no virtue in deifying the traditions of fundamentalism but at the same time they regard the answers to today's problems offered by the new evangelicals as merely tentative. One observation seems certain. If activity is a sign of life, then American evangelicalism is not yet ready for retirement.

A Long Look at NAE

This recent willingness of American conservatism to undertake an inventory of its assets and liabilities is reflected in the National Association of Evangelicals. The current leaders of NAE are well aware that certain weaknesses of the organization have appeared during its twenty-five years of service.

The early years of the Association were marked by too much reaction. Few human endeavors come into being without reaction to their antecedents, and NAE was no exception. Unfortunately, after twenty-five years many people still think of NAE in terms of an anti-ecumenical stance. For this and other reasons NAE has thus far proved incapable of gaining the support of large sections of conservative Protestantism, notably from the

Southern Baptist and Missouri Synod Lutheran ranks. NAE's apparent inability to enlist the cooperation of groups deeply rooted in the Reformation was dramatized when the Christian Reformed Church withdrew in the 1950's.

Yet, in spite of its weaknesses, as Carl F. H. Henry expresses it, "No movement has done as much to advance evangelical concerns on a trans-denominational basis, during the past twenty-five years of inclusive ecumenism, as has NAE."

The greatest accomplishment of NAE is the enlistment of more than 2,000,000 evangelicals upon a theological foundation consonant with Scripture. For two and a half decades now NAE has, by its mere existence, argued that unity in the truth is possible. "Evangelical" need no longer be a term associated with schism, discord, and rancor.

Moreover, NAE and its affiliated organizations have offered to the evangelical world a variety of services. The World Relief Commission has expressed a Christ-centered compassion for suffering humanity. The Chaplaincy Commission has provided a passage for ministers from smaller evangelical denominations into the military service. The National Sunday School Association has sparked a new enthusiasm in Christian education. The National Religious Broadcasters have elevated the ethics and strengthened the voice of evangelical radio broadcasters. The Evangelical Foreign Missions Association has assisted missionary societies in the world's trouble spots and often kept the doors of ministry open. All this and more is written large across the past quarter of a century.

As NAE faces the future, one of its brightest prospects arises from its recent openness to change, its expressed desire to face its need and find an answer. Such self-criticism is a mark of maturity. To those who have shared the leadership in the Association during the past twenty-five years the needs are all too apparent. A survey of a number of these leaders revealed at least five major needs.

Topping the list is the nagging problem of finance and promotion. "I believe NAE has done a great job," says Joseph Ryan, NAE Field Director for the Southwest Region, "and though the current cult of iconoclasts among evangelicals enjoys sniping in the guise of self-criticism and improvement, I think we have a function and a story that is not told well enough or often enough. Though I do not embrace the Madison Avenue techniques of the image makers, there is no question but that NAE lacks a clearly defined image with the constituency and even among those serving on Regional Boards!"

One of the causes of this problem is the failure of ministers to set the ministry of NAE before their churches. Donald Larson, West Central Region Field Director, points to this when he says, "I have noticed a definite breakdown of communication from NAE to the grass-root level of our church life. This comes about in part by pastors failing to relate to their people what NAE is doing as a service to them and their churches. It is, on the other hand, interesting to note that when an area representative of NAE is able to relate the activities of NAE to the people at the grass-root level we see an immediate expression of interest in our ministries."

Another major need, expressed by Dr. Arnold T. Olson, President of the Evangelical Free Church of America, concerns a weakness in NAE's organizational structure. As Dr. Olson points out, NAE is made up of (a) individuals, (b) independent congregations, (c) congregations of non-member denominations, and (d) denominations. The first three groups have actively involved themselves in the mission of NAE by an informed choice. Churches of member denominations, however, maintain only a secondhand relation to the Association. Dr. Olson feels that a new program is needed by which the congregations of the member denominations can declare their position concerning local affiliation in the NAE. Such a program is, in fact, shortly to be launched.

While the values in centralization are debatable, certain leaders of NAE feel that the Association should seek greater efficiency in operations and make more explicit the ties that bind the affiliated organizations to the National Association. Joseph Ryan stresses the need for publicizing the links of the affiliate organizations with NAE by borrowing from Acts 19:15: "NSSA I know, NRB I know, EWA I know and EFMA I know, but who is NAE?" Ryan highlights an important point. Doubtless, NAE would be greatly enhanced if it could communicate more effectively the breadth of its outreach and ministry, especially its service through its affiliated agencies.

This need is closely tied to a third, the importance of a positive program that will rally the support of evangelicals from various quarters. W. Stanley Mooneyham, who was for five years Director of Information for NAE, says, "That NAE has not reached the maximum potential envisioned for it by the founding fathers is no secret. The largely negative stance which marked its early days prevented it from catching on as a popular movement and later when this stance was corrected internally the organization continued to suffer from its earlier image."

NAE, then, must hasten what is already underway, a positive ministry to a changing and challenging world. "Any organization that is simply based upon reactions to other organizations," says Everett L. Cattell, President of Malone College, "is doomed to a short life and influence. But a great ongoing work of God can be done through NAE if the emphasis is kept positive and spiritual life remains the center of its concern."

A fourth expressed need of NAE is fresh, creative leadership. In assessing the Association, Dr. Rufus Jones, General Director of the Conservative Baptist Home Mission Society, says, "It needs dynamic, creative but mature and stable leadership." Most observers of evangelicalism in America believe that such leadership is available if NAE will seek it out. Stanley Mooneyham feels that the NAE needs to broaden the base of its leadership at both the administrative and policy-making levels.

"There is a great deal of dynamic evangelical leadership presently at the edge of NAE which needs to be actively recruited into the organization. Laymen should be given an increasing role in NAE affairs. The few laymen presently involved in NAE need to have their ranks swelled."

Leadership, of course, demands large-minded men, men with perspective and discernment. Unfortunately, men of that sort often have to move against an unbiblical stream of independency that works against the greater good. "The very liberty with which the Gospel endows Christians," says Herbert S. Mekeel of the First Presbyterian Church in Schenectady, New York, "makes them individual and causes a deep sense of independence, at least in the American atmosphere. Our tradition of religious liberty makes us careless of proper relationships with other believers of like faith." NAE leaders recognize this mood of self-interest as a big barrier to greater unity within their Association and a hindrance to wider evangelical cooperation.

The final major area of need in NAE is an in-depth study of the doctrine of the church. It should be a source of deep concern to evangelicals that, while professing faith in an infallible Bible, they have produced so few worthy works on the Biblical doctrine of the church.

There are, to be sure, reasons for this lack. Evangelicals have traditionally stressed those doctrines which bear directly upon the experience of the new birth. By rejecting the sacramental view of salvation, they have found it natural to neglect the doctrine of the church.

Furthermore, those matters touching the church, its ministry, and sacraments have been precisely that which has so often divided the followers of Christ. NAE has for twenty-five years taken the course of least resistance. Tensions are reduced by avoiding the questions which provoke differences. After a quarter of a century, however, isn't it time for evangelicals to raise again the matter of the basis of Christian unity? Can they do that without facing the question, what is the church? After two and a half decades does NAE have the maturity to struggle with the one serious doctrinal issue which is the foundation of the unity it seeks? Isn't Harold Lindsell of *Christianity Today* right when he says, "Greater unity can be achieved by more careful inquiry into the true nature of unity, more research on the nature and function of the church, and a serious effort on the part of evangelicals to separate the essential from the peripheral and join themselves together more intimately on the basis of essential truth"?

Back in 1961, while serving as Executive Director of NAE, Dr. George Ford wrote in *Inter-Com*, "It is time that evangelicals begin to say something about the true nature of the church and God's purposes for and through it. If we believe it to be a voluntary association of those who are born again by the power of God, rather than a means of salvation we should make our position clear."

The evangelical view of the church that has come down to us today is a product, not only of serious New Testament study, but of historical forces here in America. Under the impact first of toleration and then of complete religious freedom, the concept of the church held by most Protestants lost any sacramental character and became instead a voluntary association of convinced Christians for the purpose of mutual edification in the worship of God and the preaching of the gospel to the lost. With the waves of revivalism in America the idea that the church should be constituted of truly regenerated believers spread and the view of the minister as above all else a "soul winner" came to prevail in evangelical circles. The democratic idea, so pervasive in the United States, helped to spread congregationalism as the "New Testament polity" and to encourage lay participation in the life of the church. The New Testament stress on "the one body in Christ" was conceived largely in terms of a mystical, invisible body, sometimes in a way that

allowed a free display of the American spirit of independency
and the free enterprise system of rivalry and competition.

Now, isn't it time evangelicals try to disengage what is Biblical in all of this from what is simply American? The creation of
an NAE Theological Commission in Denver during the 1966
convention holds the possibility of some fruitful labor in this
direction. Regional theological convocations are at present pointing the way toward a new day, but the greatest need is a
broader forum for serious theological study within an atmosphere of trust and respect. The rewards of consecrated study
on the nature and mission of the church could have a profound
effect on the ministry of NAE because the Bible, when approached with openness, has a way of challenging our hidden,
but false, assumptions.

For example, why should evangelicals shy away from the
word "merger"? Are some of our divisions merely outdated
reflections of our racialistic, nationalistic, or sectionalistic past,
or do they spring from necessary loyalty to the Biblical doctrine
of the church? Stanley Mooneyham said recently, "A conservative theology seems in recent years to have fostered a prolifer-
ation of organizations. Some of these undoubtedly need to die a
godly death in a selfless merger which would increase effec-
tiveness as well as eliminate duplication of effort." That idea
calls for serious and devout study.

A similar bold suggestion came from the recent Congress on
the Church's Worldwide Mission. Moreover, actual discussions
"to explore the possibilities of church federation" are already
underway in the National Holiness Association. The President
of the Association, Paul L. Kindschi, feels that this action will
eventually lead to organic union of most of the groups within
the organization. A similar step was taken by the Reformed
Presbyterian Church, Evangelical Synod, in May 1966, when it
moved to enter into relations with the Orthodox Presbyterian
Church to explore possible bases of union.

As evangelicals have made abundantly clear so often, merger

per se is not equivalent to true Christian unity. But isn't it time to ask if, given the right bases, unity in the sense of union may not at times be the will of God?

Take another example of the need for serious study of the doctrine of the church, the relation between "invisible" and "visible" church. What do we mean by this terminology, which is never found in Scripture? How much of this distinction rests upon Greek ideas of the "real" and how much rests upon solid Biblical exegesis? Does the Bible allow us to be irresponsible for the divisions in the "visible" church by retreating to the unity of the "invisible" church?

Surely there is significance in the fact that the Evangelical Alliance's statement of faith in 1846 included an article on the obligation and perpetuity of the ordinances of Baptism and the Lord's Supper, while the NAE statement in 1943 was content to refer to the spiritual unity of all true believers.

Or again, take the example of the "pure" church. What do we mean by the purity or the holiness of the church? A totally regenerated membership? Biblical standards of belief and practice? Or a withdrawn assembly of believers in an apostate age awaiting Christ's imminent return?

All of these questions, and more, lie at the very foundation of the evangelical quest for unity in our day. Our plea here is not for universal agreement on all of these questions. True unity will continue to be more of a matter of the heart than of the head, more of attitude than of answers. But the Christian virtue of honesty demands that we properly reflect on the views of those with whom we differ. And the evangelical conviction touching the authority of Scripture demands that we continually bring our views to the test of what "stands written." Stagnation begins in an organization, as in a pool, when movement ceases, when questions no longer trouble the waters.

Evangelicals must avoid, on the one hand, the attitude of the iconoclast who criticizes and destroys just for the satisfaction of feeling superior and, on the other hand, the attitude of defensiveness that assumes that all the answers are in.

The Strength of Evangelicalism

In conclusion, then, what can we say on the twenty-fifth anniversary of NAE about the strength of evangelicalism in America today. No simple answer to that question can be given. Since evangelicalism, as we have seen, is by nature dynamic and personal, it cannot be identified with any single institution or group of churches. But, then, what sort of index would one use? The membership rolls of the Southern Baptist Convention? The circulation of *Christianity Today?* The attendance at Billy Graham crusades? In his recent *Religion in America* Winthrop S. Hudson estimates that the "Fundamentalist-Adventist-Holiness-Pentecostal coalition" numbers about 8,500,000 and that Southern Baptists plus the American Lutheran Church and the Lutheran Church, Missouri Synod, account for 19,000,000 more outside of the "cooperative Protestantism" of the National Council of Churches. In 1966 Dr. John A. MacKay estimated that a quarter to a third of the total membership of the conciliar churches is evangelical. While these figures may be helpful in showing relative strengths, there is simply no statistical way of tabulating the influence of evangelicalism.

That does not mean, however, that we can draw no conclusions about its present condition. One fact above all others seems obvious. Twentieth-century evangelicalism in the United States has not been able to hold the gains of its nineteenth-century counterpart. The general secular mood of our time, fed by our urbanized, industrialized cities, has eaten away at the heart of evangelical thinking and action. For influence upon American society the circuit-riding Methodist preacher and the rail-splitting Baptist farmer-pastor have no successor. This is not because evangelicals have shunned the printed page, radio, or highly publicized evangelistic campaigns. These and other modern methods have propagated the Biblical witness, but the frigid facts are that the evangelical voice no longer sounds from the centers of national life, from Washington, Wall Street, and Hollywood.

On the other hand, because the mass media in the United States project a secularized liberal image of tolerance and goodwill called "the American way," the uninformed are likely to underestimate evangelicalism's strength. The vigor of conservative Christianity in the United States can be glimpsed in a number of ways:

(1) The continuing high proportion of Americans who confess a tip-of-the-hat belief in the cardinal Christian doctrines is largely due to the afterglow of a bright evangelical past in this country. While the figures may be declining, poll after poll points to the average American's belief in God, in the Bible, in hell, and in the other basic articles of the Christian creed. Much of this is attributable to the revivalistic success of evangelicalism in an earlier day in the United States.

(2) Evangelical Christians can be found in nearly every Protestant denomination. While in most major Protestant bodies this witness has been greatly compromised or muffled in the last century, a few of the larger denominations continue almost totally conservative in theological stance—the Southern Baptists and the Missouri Synod Lutherans are two prominent examples—and smaller bodies such as the Christian Reformed Church relate evangelical principles to their own distinctive testimony.

This pervasiveness of Biblical Christianity should guard the careful observer of today's religious scene from two erroneous generalizations. It should keep him, on the one hand, from identifying evangelicalism with fundamentalism. The tendency of fundamentalism to seek independent channels has diverted it from the main stream of most major denominations, especially those drawing deeply from the wells of the Protestant Reformation. On the other hand, it should also keep the observer from using "evangelical" and "ecumenical" as antithetical terms. Since the fact of the matter is that many of the denominations affiliated with the National Council of Churches and the World Council of Churches include numbers of evangelical congregations, one cannot in fairness equate evangelical with separatist. That is a mistake too often made among American conservatives. Accuracy requires some other distinctions such as conciliar (NCC and WCC) ecumenists and conservative evangelicals.

(3) The primary evidence of evangelicalism's vigor still lies in those twins of her early years, evangelism and missions. The story of Billy Graham's meteoric rise to global significance is a familiar one. There is no need to rehearse it here. What may not always be evident, however, is the high degree of success Dr. Graham's organization has had in rallying evangelical forces. The roster of churches supporting any given campaign may well be the best index yet of the evangelical strength in that community. He draws not only from the churches of the NAE constituency but from Southern Baptists, Lutherans of various synods, a few Episcopal churches, an assortment of Independents, a Methodist church here and there, Presbyterians, Disciples, and even occasionally individual Roman Catholics. When forty or fifty thousand people crowd into a football stadium in Boston or Denver or San Francisco on a Sunday afternoon, one begins to realize that evangelicalism in America is far from dead.

In recent days we have seen this evangelistic concern thrust into the international scene by the World Congress on Evangelism (October 26-November 4, 1966) in Berlin's Kongresshalle. Over 1,100 delegates from more than 100 countries gathered not far from the Berlin wall to define and clarify Biblical evangelism for our day, to underline its urgency in the present situation, to challenge the church to renew its own life through an intensified proclamation of the historic faith, and to show the world in a fresh and dramatic way that God is in truth Lord of all, and that He saves men through His Son.

Though the Congress revealed again the lack of evangelical consensus on the relation of evangelism to social action, it provided at the same time an impressive example of Christian unity based on a common concern to evangelize the world. Churchmen from long-established communions joined with newly converted Auca Indians in prayer, praise, and fellowship.

While evangelism now and then captures the headlines, the strength of the evangelical missionary enterprise is not always appreciated. Due to the publicized activities of the National Council of Churches, the World Council of Churches and their missionary departments, one could easily get the impression that conservative missionary endeavor is limited to a handful of "faith" missions. The facts are quite to the contrary.

Fortunately, two recent developments have combined to bring the vitality of evangelical missions before the religious public. The first is the missionary heroism and drama surrounding the Auca martyrdoms in 1956 and the more recent slaughters in the Congo. Jim Elliot, Paul Carlson, Irene Farel, and the other modern martyrs have added luster to the missionary calling and focused world attention, at least for a time, upon the usually unnoticed disciples of Jesus Christ. The eagerness of major publishers to get these stories before the reading public has contributed no little to recent interest in evangelical missions.

The second development is the recent series of giant conferences sponsored by evangelicals and devoted to the missionary task. The student gatherings at the Urbana campus of the University of Illinois during the Christmas holidays are good illustrations of this. These student conventions, sponsored by Inter-Varsity Christian Fellowship, draw up to 7,000 students every four years to hear addresses by evangelical leaders and to converse informally with missionary spokesmen. One cannot join the 7,000 collegians in singing "To God Be the Glory" without sensing something of the vigor of this Christian student movement.

Of even greater import, because it involved a greater portion of the missionary task force, was the recent Congress on the Church's Worldwide Mission. The spirit of unity that pervaded the Congress was a small miracle in itself. The delegates represented those missions affiliated with the Evangelical Foreign Missions Association and the Interdenominational Foreign Missions Association. Combined, the two associations represent nearly 13,000 missionaries, two-fifths of North America's Protestant missionary force. Naturally, the doctrinal tensions of conservative Christianity, including dispensationalism, pentecostalism, and ecclesiology, were potentially disruptive, but the bonds of fellowship and the missionary concern proved more than able to withstand those tensions. The Wheaton Congress may well herald a new day for interdenominational evangelicalism.

No one, then, can with certainty measure the strength of American evangelicalism today. God works in hidden ways to accomplish His saving purposes. The sympathetic observer is struck by evangelicalism's theological vigor, its missionary passion, its openness to new ministries, and its awakening mood of repentance for the wounded body of Christ. Many evangelicals must still outgrow their organizational naïveté and face up to the importance of unified effort, but the future of American evangelicalism is by no means dark. As long as contemporary men continue to stagger in their materialistic and nihilistic stupor, the authoritative Word sounded in evangelicalism will be needed to point the way to freedom, life and immortality.

Notes

CHAPTER 1

A. Skevington Wood's *The Inextinguishable Blaze* (Grand Rapids: Eerdmans, 1960) is a good introduction to the evangelical awakening in England. Several of Wesley's quotations and the views of Whitefield expressed in this chapter can be found in Wood's book. A survey of Wesley's doctrine is contained in *A Compend of Wesley's Theology* edited by Robert W. Burtner and Robert E. Chiles (New York: Abingdon, 1954). Wesley's views on sin and the Bible expressed in this chapter are developed further in Burtner and Chiles' volume.

Kierkegaard's quotation in this chapter is from his *Attack Upon 'Christendom'* (Boston: Beacon Press, 1956), p. 274.

W. Curry Mavis' words are from his *Beyond Conformity* (Winona Lake: Light and Life, 1958), p. 87, and Professor Latourette's view is from his *Anno Domini* (New York: Harper, 1940), p. 169.

The missionary verse is Reginald Heber's widely sung hymn "From Greenland's Icy Mountains."

CHAPTER 2

Whitefield's Philadelphia courthouse sermon is quoted in William Warren Sweet's *The Story of Religion in America* (New York: Harper, 1950), pp. 141-142.

Puritanism has received much attention from scholars. One of the better introductions is William Haller's *The Rise of Puritanism* (New York: Harper, 1957). Two helpful general surveys of the movements discussed in this chapter are A. C. McGiffert's *Protestant Thought Before Kant* (New York: Scribner's, 1926) and *Protestant Christianity* by John Dillenberger and Claude Welch (New York: Scribner's, 1954).

The quotation concerning Spurgeon's preaching in this chapter is from *The Christian's World* and is quoted in A. C. Underwood's *A History of the English Baptists* (London: Carey Kingsgate, 1956), p. 220.

CHAPTER 3

The standard source for the study of American Christianity is a two-volume work *American Christianity* by H. Shelton Smith, Robert T. Handy and Lefferts A. Loetscher (New York: Scribner's, 1963). Winthrop S. Hudson has become the dean of American church historians since the publication of his excellent *Religion in America* (New York: Scribner's, 1965). Much of the material in this chapter is drawn from this, his latest work. His *American Protestantism* (Chicago: Chicago University Press, 1961), however, is also very helpful, especially in its discussion of denominationalism.

Another insightful discussion of American evangelicalism is Sidney Mead's chapter "The Rise of the Evangelical Concept of the Ministry in America" in *The Ministry in Historical Perspective* edited by H. Richard Niebuhr and Daniel D. Williams (New York: Harper, 1956).

The discussion of the Princeton view of inspiration found in this chapter is drawn from Ernest R. Sandeen's "The Princeton Theology" in *Church History*, XXXI, No. 3 (September, 1962), pp. 307-321.

CHAPTER 4

The addresses and actions of the St. Louis conference on United Action among Evangelicals are all recorded in *Evangelical Action* (Boston: United Action Press, 1942), edited by the NAE Executive Committee.

The standard history of the early years of NAE is James DeForest Murch's *Cooperation Without Compromise* (Grand Rapids: Eerdmans, 1956).

CHAPTER 5

The history and ministry of NAE in this chapter is drawn almost completely from the pages of *United Evangelical Action* and from reports of the NAE conventions.

CHAPTER 6

Arnold W. Hearn's article "Fundamentalist Renascence" is in *The Christian Century*, April 30, 1958, p. 528, while A. W. Tozer's remarks about fundamentalism are from an interview which appeared in *Christian Life*, "Can Fundamentalism Be Saved?" by David Enlow, August 1954, pp. 14-16.

Harold John Ockenga's "Resurgent Evangelical Leadership" is in *Christianity Today*, October 10, 1960. Permission to quote from this article was kindly granted by *Christianity Today*. Professor Furniss' remarks are in his *The Fundamentalist Controversy 1918-1931* (New Haven, Conn.: Yale University Press, 1954), pp. 38-39. The more recent developments within fundamentalism have been ably discussed by Louis Gasper in his *The Fundamentalist Movement* (The Hague: Moulton, 1963).

Carl F. H. Henry's views on "The Perils of Independency" are from *Christianity Today*, November 12, 1956, p. 20. The whole subject of "the new evangelicalism" is treated by Ronald H. Nash in his *The New Evangelicalism* (Grand Rapids: Zondervan, 1963).